SELECTED POEMS

BY

W. B. YEATS

SELECTED POEMS
LYRICAL AND NARRATIVE
BY
W. B. YEATS

MACMILLAN AND CO., LIMITED
ST. MARTIN'S STREET, LONDON
1951

PRINTED IN GREAT BRITAIN

PREFACE

I HAVE arranged in chronological order whatever lyrical and narrative poems of mine best please my friends or myself, or best illuminate one another. Though I have often in these last thirty years corrected the earliest, I leave all, even two in "The Rose" that are almost wholly new, in their original context, for all belong in thought and sentiment to the time when they were first written.

W. B. Y.

MAY 1929.

v

CONTENTS

ix

FROM "MICHAEL ROBARTES AND THE DANCER" (1921)

FROM "THE TOWER" (1928)

THE WANDERINGS OF USHEEN

(1889)

BOOK I

S. PATRIC

You who are bent, and bald, and blind,
With a heavy heart and a wandering mind,
Have known three centuries, poets sing,
Of dalliance with a demon thing.

USHEEN

Sad to remember, sick with years,
The swift innumerable spears,
The horsemen with their floating hair,
And bowls of barley, honey, and wine,
Those merry couples dancing in tune,
And the white body that lay by mine;
But the tale, though words be lighter than air,
Must live to be old like the wandering moon.

Caolte, and Conan, and Finn were there,
When we followed a deer with our baying hounds,
With Bran, Sgeolan, and Lomair,
And passing the Firbolgs' burial mounds,
Came to the cairn-heaped grassy hill
Where passionate Maive is stony still;
And found on the dove-grey edge of the sea
A pearl-pale, high-born lady, who rode
On a horse with bridle of findrinny;
And like a sunset were her lips,
A stormy sunset on doomed ships;
A citron colour gloomed in her hair,
But down to her feet white vesture flowed,
And with the glimmering crimson glowed

3

Of many a figured embroidery ;
And it was bound with a pearl-pale shell
That wavered like the summer streams,
As her soft bosom rose and fell.

S. PATRIC

You are still wrecked among heathen dreams.

USHEEN

" Why do you wind no horn ? " she said,
" And every hero droop his head ?
The hornless deer is not more sad
That many a peaceful moment had,
More sleek than any granary mouse,
In his own leafy forest house
Among the waving fields of fern :
The hunting of heroes should be glad."

" O pleasant woman," answered Finn,
" We think on Oscar's pencilled urn,
And on the heroes lying slain,
On Gavra's raven-covered plain ;
But where are your noble kith and kin,
And from what country do you ride ? "

" My father and my mother are
Aengus and Adene, my own name
Niam, and my country far
Beyond the tumbling of this tide."

" What dream came with you that you came
Through bitter tide on foam-wet feet ?

Did your companion wander away
From where the birds of Aengus wing ? "

Thereon did she look haughty and sweet :
" I have not yet, war-weary king,
Been spoken of with any man ;
Yet now I choose, for these four feet
Ran through the foam and ran to this
That I might have your son to kiss."

" Were there no better than my son
That you through all that foam should run ? "

" I loved no man, though kings besought,
Until the Danaan poets brought
Rhyme, that rhymed to Usheen's name,
And now I am dizzy with the thought
Of all that wisdom and the fame
Of battles broken by his hands,
Of stories builded by his words
That are like coloured Asian birds
At evening in their rainless lands."

O Patric, by your brazen bell,
There was no limb of mine but fell
Into a desperate gulph of love !
" You only will I wed," I cried,
" And I will make a thousand songs,
And set your name all names above,
And captives bound with leathern thongs
Shall kneel and praise you, one by one,
At evening in my western dun."

B   5

" O Usheen, mount by me and ride
To shores by the wash of the tremulous tide,
Where men have heaped no burial mounds,
And the days pass by like a wayward tune,
Where broken faith has never been known,
And the blushes of first love never have flown ;
And there I will give you a hundred hounds ;
No mightier creatures bay at the moon ;
And a hundred robes of murmuring silk,
And a hundred calves and a hundred sheep
Whose long wool whiter than sea-froth flows,
And a hundred spears and a hundred bows,
And oil and wine and honey and milk,
And always never-anxious sleep ;
While a hundred youths, mighty of limb,
But knowing nor tumult nor hate nor strife,
And a hundred ladies, merry as birds,
Who when they dance to a fitful measure
Have a speed like the speed of the salmon herds,
Shall follow your horn and obey your whim,
And you shall know the Danaan leisure :
And Niam be with you for a wife."
Then she sighed gently, " It grows late,
Music and love and sleep await,
Where I would be when the white moon climbs,
The red sun falls and the world grows dim."

And then I mounted and she bound me
With her triumphing arms around me,
And whispering to herself enwound me ;
But when the horse had felt my weight,
He shook himself and neighed three times :
Caolte, Conan, and Finn came near,

And wept, and raised their lamenting hands,
And bid me stay, with many a tear;
But we rode out from the human lands.

In what far kingdom do you go,
Ah, Fenians, with the shield and bow?
Or are you phantoms white as snow,
Whose lips had life's most prosperous glow?
O you, with whom in sloping valleys,
Or down the dewy forest alleys,
I chased at morn the flying deer,
With whom I hurled the hurrying spear,
And heard the foemen's bucklers rattle,
And broke the heaving ranks of battle!
And Bran, Sgeolan, and Lomair,
Where are you with your long rough hair?
You go not where the red deer feeds,
Nor tear the foemen from their steeds.

S. PATRIC

Boast not, nor mourn with drooping head
Companions long accurst and dead,
And hounds for centuries dust and air.

USHEEN

We galloped over the glossy sea:
I know not if days passed or hours,
And Niam sang continually
Danaan songs, and their dewy showers
Of pensive laughter, unhuman sound,
Lulled weariness, and softly round
My human sorrow her white arms wound.

7

We galloped ; now a hornless deer
Passed by us, chased by a phantom hound
All pearly white, save one red ear ;
And now a lady rode like the wind
With an apple of gold in her tossing hand ;
And a beautiful young man followed behind
With quenchless gaze and fluttering hair.

" Were these two born in the Danaan land,
Or have they breathed the mortal air ? "

" Vex them no longer," Niam said,
And sighing bowed her gentle head,
And sighing laid the pearly tip
Of one long finger on my lip.

But now the moon like a white rose shone
In the pale west, and the sun's rim sank,
And clouds arrayed their rank on rank
About his fading crimson ball :
The floor of Allen's hosting hall
Was not more level than the sea,
As full of loving phantasy,
And with low murmurs we rode on,
Where many a trumpet-twisted shell
That in immortal silence sleeps
Dreaming of her own melting hues,
Her golds, her ambers, and her blues,
Pierced with soft light the shallowing deeps.
But now a wandering land breeze came
And a far sound of feathery quires ;
It seemed to blow from the dying flame,
They seemed to sing in the smouldering fires.
The horse towards the music raced,

Neighing along the lifeless waste ;
Like sooty fingers, many a tree
Rose ever out of the warm sea ;
And they were trembling ceaselessly,
As though they all were beating time,
Upon the centre of the sun,
To that low laughing woodland rhyme.
And, now our wandering hours were done,
We cantered to the shore, and knew
The reason of the trembling trees :
Round every branch the song-birds flew,
Or clung thereon like swarming bees ;
While round the shore a million stood
Like drops of frozen rainbow light,
And pondered in a soft vain mood
Upon their shadows in the tide,
And told the purple deeps their pride,
And murmured snatches of delight ;
And on the shores were many boats
With bending sterns and bending bows,
And carven figures on their prows
Of bitterns, and fish-eating stoats,
And swans with their exultant throats :
And where the wood and waters meet
We tied the horse in a leafy clump,
And Niam blew three merry notes
Out of a little silver trump ;
And then an answering whispering flew
Over the bare and woody land,
A whisper of impetuous feet,
And ever nearer, nearer grew ;
And from the woods rushed out a band
Of men and ladies, hand in hand,

And singing, singing all together ;
Their brows were white as fragrant milk,
Their cloaks made out of yellow silk,
And trimmed with many a crimson feather ;
And when they saw the cloak I wore
Was dim with mire of a mortal shore,
They fingered it and gazed on me
And laughed like murmurs of the sea ;
But Niam with a swift distress
Bid them away and hold their peace ;
And when they heard her voice they ran
And knelt there, every girl and man
And kissed, as they would never cease,
Her pearl-pale hand and the hem of her dress.
She bade them bring us to the hall
Where Aengus dreams, from sun to sun,
A Druid dream of the end of days
When the stars are to wane and the world be done.

They led us by long and shadowy ways
Where drops of dew in myriads fall,
And tangled creepers every hour
Blossom in some new crimson flower,
And once a sudden laughter sprang
From all their lips, and once they sang
Together, while the dark woods rang,
And made in all their distant parts,
With boom of bees in honey marts,
A rumour of delighted hearts.
And once a lady by my side
Gave me a harp, and bid me sing,
And touch the laughing silver string ;
But when I sang of human joy

A sorrow wrapped each merry face,
And, Patric ! by your beard, they wept,
Until one came, a tearful boy ;
" A sadder creature never stept
Than this strange human bard," he cried ;
And caught the silver harp away,
And, weeping over the white strings, hurled
It down in a leaf-hid, hollow place
That kept dim waters from the sky ;
And each one said, with a long, long sigh,
" O saddest harp in all the world,
Sleep there till the moon and the stars die ! "

And now still sad we came to where
A beautiful young man dreamed within
A house of wattles, clay, and skin ;
One hand upheld his beardless chin,
And one a sceptre flashing out
Wild flames of red and gold and blue,
Like to a merry wandering rout
Of dancers leaping in the air ;
And men and ladies knelt them there
And showed their eyes with teardrops dim,
And with low murmurs prayed to him,
And kissed the sceptre with red lips,
And touched it with their finger-tips.

He held that flashing sceptre up.
" Joy drowns the twilight in the dew,
And fills with stars night's purple cup,
And wakes the sluggard seeds of corn,
And stirs the young kid's budding horn
And makes the infant ferns unwrap,

And for the peewit paints his cap,
And rolls along the unwieldy sun,
And makes the little planets run :
And if joy were not on the earth,
There were an end of change and birth,
And Earth and Heaven and Hell would die,
And in some gloomy barrow lie
Folded like a frozen fly ;
Then mock at Death and Time with glances
And wavering arms and wandering dances.

" Men's hearts of old were drops of flame
That from the saffron morning came,
Or drops of silver joy that fell
Out of the moon's pale twisted shell ;
But now hearts cry that hearts are slaves,
And toss and turn in narrow caves ;
But here there is nor law nor rule,
Nor have hands held a weary tool ;
And here there is nor Change nor Death,
But only kind and merry breath,
For joy is God and God is joy."
With one long glance for girl and boy
And the pale blossom of the moon,
He fell into a Druid swoon.

And in a wild and sudden dance
We mocked at Time and Fate and Chance
And swept out of the wattled hall
And came to where the dewdrops fall
Among the foamdrops of the sea,
And there we hushed the revelry ;
And, gathering on our brows a frown,
Bent all our swaying bodies down,

And to the waves that glimmer by
That sloping green De Danaan sod
Sang, " God is joy and joy is God.
And things that have grown sad are wicked,
And things that fear the dawn of the morrow
Or the grey wandering osprey Sorrow."

We danced to where in the winding thicket
The damask roses, bloom on bloom,
Like crimson meteors hang in the gloom,
And bending over them softly said,
Bending over them in the dance,
With a swift and friendly glance
From dewy eyes : " Upon the dead
Fall the leaves of other roses,
On the dead dim earth encloses :
But never, never on our graves,
Heaped beside the glimmering waves,
Shall fall the leaves of damask roses.
For neither Death nor Change comes near us,
And all listless hours fear us,
And we fear no dawning morrow,
Nor the grey wandering osprey Sorrow."

The dance wound through the windless woods ;
The ever-summered solitudes ;
Until the tossing arms grew still
Upon the woody central hill ;
And, gathered in a panting band,
We flung on high each waving hand,
And sang unto the starry broods.
In our raised eyes there flashed a glow
Of milky brightness to and fro

As thus our song arose: "You stars,
Across your wandering ruby cars
Shake the loose reins: you slaves of God,
He rules you with an iron rod,
He holds you with an iron bond,
Each one woven to the other,
Each one woven to his brother
Like bubbles in a frozen pond;
But we in a lonely land abide
Unchainable as the dim tide,
With hearts that know nor law nor rule,
And hands that hold no wearisome tool,
Folded in love that fears no morrow,
Nor the grey wandering osprey Sorrow."

O Patric! for a hundred years
I chased upon that woody shore
The deer, the badger, and the boar.
O Patric! for a hundred years
At evening on the glimmering sands,
Beside the piled-up hunting spears,
These now outworn and withered hands
Wrestled among the island bands.
O Patric! for a hundred years
We went a-fishing in long boats
With bending sterns and bending bows,
And carven figures on their prows
Of bitterns and fish-eating stoats.
O Patric! for a hundred years
The gentle Niam was my wife;
But now two things devour my life;
The things that most of all I hate;
Fasting and prayers.

S. PATRIC

Tell on.

USHEEN

Yes, yes,
For these were ancient Usheen's fate
Loosed long ago from Heaven's gate,
For his last days to lie in wait.

When one day by the tide I stood,
I found in that forgetfulness
Of dreamy foam a staff of wood
From some dead warrior's broken lance :
I turned it in my hands ; the stains
Of war were on it, and I wept,
Remembering how the Fenians stept
Along the blood-bedabbled plains,
Equal to good or grievous chance :
Thereon young Niam softly came
And caught my hands, but spake no word
Save only many times my name,
In murmurs, like a frighted bird.
We passed by woods, and lawns of clover,
And found the horse and bridled him,
For we knew well the old was over.
I heard one say, " His eyes grow dim
With all the ancient sorrow of men " ;
And wrapped in dreams rode out again
With hoofs of the pale findrinny
Over the glimmering purple sea :
Under the golden evening light.

The immortals moved among the fountains
By rivers and the woods' old night;
Some danced like shadows on the mountains,
Some wandered ever hand in hand;
Or sat in dreams on the pale strand,
Each forehead like an obscure star
Bent down above each hooked knee,
And sang, and with a dreamy gaze
Watched where the sun in a saffron blaze
Was slumbering half in the sea-ways;
And, as they sang, the painted birds
Kept time with their bright wings and feet;
Like drops of honey came their words,
But fainter than a young lamb's bleat.

" An old man stirs the fire to a blaze,
In the house of a child, of a friend, of a brother
He has over-lingered his welcome; the days,
Grown desolate, whisper and sigh to each other;
He hears the storm in the chimney above,
And bends to the fire and shakes with the cold,
While his heart still dreams of battle and love,
And the cry of the hounds on the hills of old.

" But we are apart in the grassy places,
Where care cannot trouble the least of our days,
Or the softness of youth be gone from our faces,
Or love's first tenderness die in our gaze.
The hare grows old as she plays in the sun
And gazes around her with eyes of brightness;
Before the swift things that she dreamed of were done
She limps along in an aged whiteness;
A storm of birds in the Asian trees

Like tulips in the air a-winging,
And the gentle waves of the summer seas,
That raise their heads and wander singing,
Must murmur at last ' Unjust, unjust ';
And ' My speed is a weariness,' falters the mouse,
And the kingfisher turns to a ball of dust,
And the roof falls in of his tunnelled house.
But the love-dew dims our eyes till the day
When God shall come from the sea with a sigh
And bid the stars drop down from the sky,
And the moon like a pale rose wither away."

BOOK II

Now, man of croziers, shadows called our names
And then away, away, like whirling flames ;
And now fled by, mist-covered, without sound,
The youth and lady and the deer and hound ;
" Gaze no more on the phantoms," Niam said,
And kissed my eyes, and, swaying her bright head
And her bright body, sang of faery and man
Before God was or my old line began ;
Wars shadowy, vast, exultant ; faeries of old
Who wedded men with rings of Druid gold ;
And how those lovers never turn their eyes
Upon the life that fades and flickers and dies,
Yet love and kiss on dim shores far away
Rolled round with music of the sighing spray :
Yet sang no more, as when, like a brown bee
That has drunk full, she crossed the misty sea
With me in her white arms a hundred years
Before this day ; for now the fall of tears
Troubled her song.
                    I do not know if days
Or hours passed by, yet hold the morning rays
Shone many times among the glimmering flowers
Woven into her hair, before dark towers
Rose in the darkness, and the white surf gleamed
About them ; and the horse of faery screamed
And shivered, knowing the Isle of Many Fears,
Nor ceased until white Niam stroked his ears
And named him by sweet names.
                              A foaming tide
Whitened afar with surge, fan-formed and wide,
Burst from a great door marred by many a blow

From mace and sword and pole-axe, long ago
When gods and giants warred.   We rode between
The seaweed-covered pillars ; and the green
And surging phosphorus alone gave light
On our dark pathway, till a countless flight
Of moonlit steps glimmered ; and left and right
Dark statues glimmered over the pale tide
Upon dark thrones.   Between the lids of one
The imaged meteors had flashed and run
And had disported in the stilly jet,
And the fixed stars had dawned and shone and set,
Since God made Time and Death and Sleep : the
    other
Stretched his long arm to where, a misty smother,
The stream churned, churned, and churned—his lips
    apart,
As though he told his never-slumbering heart
Of every foamdrop on its misty way.
Tying the horse to his vast foot that lay
Half in the unvesselled sea, we climbed the stairs
And climbed so long, I thought the last steps were
Hung from the morning star ; when these mild
    words
Fanned the delighted air like wings of birds :
" My brothers spring out of their beds at morn,
A-murmur like young partridge : with loud horn
They chase the noontide deer ;
And when the dew-drowned stars hang in the air
Look to long fishing-lines, or point and pare
An ashen hunting spear.
O sigh, O fluttering sigh, be kind to me ;
Flutter along the froth lips of the sea,
And shores, the froth lips wet :

19

And stay a little while, and bid them weep :
Ah, touch their blue-veined eyelids if they sleep,
And shake their coverlet.
When you have told how I weep endlessly,
Flutter along the froth lips of the sea
And home to me again,
And in the shadow of my hair lie hid,
And tell me that you found a man unbid,
The saddest of all men."

A lady with soft eyes like funeral tapers,
And face that seemed wrought out of moonlit
    vapours,
And a sad mouth, that fear made tremulous
As any ruddy moth, looked down on us ;
And she with a wave-rusted chain was tied
To two old eagles, full of ancient pride,
That with dim eyeballs stood on either side.
Few feathers were on their dishevelled wings,
For their dim minds were with the ancient things.

" I bring deliverance," pearl-pale Niam said.

" Neither the living, nor the unlabouring dead,
Nor the high gods who never lived, may fight
My enemy and hope ; demons for fright
Jabber and scream about him in the night ;
For he is strong and crafty as the seas
That sprang under the Seven Hazel Trees,
And I must needs endure and hate and weep,
Until the gods and demons drop asleep,
Hearing Aed touch the mournful strings of gold."

" Is he so dreadful ? "

                    " Be not over bold,
But fly while still you may."

                        And thereon I :
" This demon shall be battered till he die,
And his loose bulk be thrown in the loud tide."

" Flee from him," pearl-pale Niam weeping cried,
" For all men flee the demons " ; but moved not
My angry king-remembering soul one jot.
There was no mightier soul of Heber's line ;
Now it is old and mouse-like.   For a sign
I burst the chain : still earless, nerveless, blind,
Wrapped in the things of the unhuman mind,
In some dim memory or ancient mood
Still earless, nerveless, blind, the eagles stood.

And then we climbed the stair to a high door ;
A hundred horsemen on the basalt floor
Beneath had paced content : we held our way
And stood within : clothed in a misty ray
I saw a foam-white seagull drift and float
Under the roof, and with a straining throat
Shouted, and hailed him : he hung there a star,
For no man's cry shall ever mount so far ;
Not even your God could have thrown down that
    hall ;
Stabling His unloosed lightnings in their stall,
He had sat down and sighed with cumbered heart,
As though His hour were come.

                      We sought the part
That was most distant from the door ; green slime

Made the way slippery, and time on time
Showed prints of sea-born scales, while down
    through it
The captive's journeys to and fro were writ
Like a small river, and where feet touched, came
A momentary gleam of phosphorus flame.
Under the deepest shadows of the hall
That woman found a ring hung on the wall,
And in the ring a torch, and with its flare
Making a world about her in the air,
Passed under the dim doorway, out of sight
And came again, holding a second light
Burning between her fingers, and in mine
Laid it and sighed : I held a sword whose shine
No centuries could dim, and a word ran
Thereon in Ogham letters, " Mananan " ;
That sea-god's name, who in a deep content
Sprang dripping, and, with captive demons sent
Out of the sevenfold seas, built the dark hall
Rooted in foam and clouds, and cried to all
The mightier masters of a mightier race ;
And at his cry there came no milk-pale face
Under a crown of thorns and dark with blood,
But only exultant faces.

                  Niam stood
With bowed head, trembling when the white blade
    shone,
But she whose hours of tenderness were gone
Had neither hope nor fear.   I bade them hide
Under the shadows till the tumults died
Of the loud-crashing and earth-shaking fight,
Lest they should look upon some dreadful sight ;

And thrust the torch between the slimy flags.
A dome made out of endless carven jags,
Where shadowy face flowed into shadowy face,
Looked down on me ; and in the self-same place
I waited hour by hour, and the high dome,
Windowless, pillarless, multitudinous home
Of faces, waited ; and the leisured gaze
Was loaded with the memory of days
Buried and mighty.   When through the great door
The dawn came in, and glimmered on the floor
With a pale light, I journeyed round the hall
And found a door deep sunken in the wall,
The least of doors ; beyond on a dim plain
A little runnel made a bubbling strain,
And on the runnel's stony and bare edge
A dusky demon dry as a withered sedge
Swayed, crooning to himself an unknown tongue :
In a sad revelry he sang and swung
Bacchant and mournful, passing to and fro
His hand along the runnel's side, as though
The flowers still grew there : far on the sea's waste
Shaking and waving, vapour vapour chased,
While high frail cloudlets, fed with a green light,
Like drifts of leaves, immovable and bright,
Hung in the passionate dawn.   He slowly turned :
A demon's leisure : eyes, first white, now burned
Like wings of kingfishers ; and he arose
Barking.   We trampled up and down with blows
Of sword and brazen battle-axe, while day
Gave to high noon and noon to night gave way ;
And when he knew the sword of Mananan
Amid the shades of night, he changed and ran
Through many shapes ; I lunged at the smooth throat

23

Of a great eel ; it changed, and I but smote
A fir-tree roaring in its leafless top ;
And thereupon I drew the livid chop
Of a drowned dripping body to my breast ;
Horror from horror grew ; but when the west
Had surged up in a plumy fire, I drave
Through heart and spine ; and cast him in the wave
Lest Niam shudder.

                  Full of hope and dread
Those two came carrying wine and meat and
    bread,
And healed my wounds with unguents out of flowers
That feed white moths by some De Danaan shrine ;
Then in that hall, lit by the dim sea-shine,
We lay on skins of otters, and drank wine,
Brewed by the sea-gods, from huge cups that lay
Upon the lips of sea-gods in their day ;
And then on heaped-up skins of otters slept.
And when the sun once more in saffron stept,
Rolling his flagrant wheel out of the deep,
We sang the loves and angers without sleep,
And all the exultant labours of the strong.

But now the lying clerics murder song
With barren words and flatteries of the weak.
In what land do the powerless turn the beak
Of ravening Sorrow, or the hand of Wrath ?
For all your croziers, they have left the path
And wander in the storms and clinging snows,
Hopeless for ever : ancient Usheen knows,
For he is weak and poor and blind, and lies
On the anvil of the world.

                    Be still : the skies
Are choked with thunder, lightning, and fierce wind,
For God has heard, and speaks His angry mind ;
Go cast your body on the stones and pray,
For He has wrought midnight and dawn and day.

USHEEN

Saint, do you weep ?   I hear amid the thunder
The Fenian horses ; armour torn asunder ;
Laughter and cries.   The armies clash and shock.
And now the daylight-darkening ravens flock.
Cease, cease, oh mournful, laughing Fenian horn !

We feasted for three days.   On the fourth morn
I found, dropping sea foam on the wide stair,
And hung with slime, and whispering in his hair,
That demon dull and unsubduable ;
And once more to a day-long battle fell,
And at the sundown threw him in the surge,
To lie until the fourth morn saw emerge
His new-healed shape ; and for a hundred years
So warred, so feasted, with nor dreams nor fears,
Nor languor nor fatigue : an endless feast,
An endless war.

                    The hundred years had ceased ;
I stood upon the stair : the surges bore
A beech bough to me, and my heart grew sore,
Remembering how I had stood by white-haired Finn
Under a beech at Allen and heard the thin
Outcry of bats.

And then young Niam came
Holding that horse, and sadly called my name ;
I mounted, and we passed over the lone
And drifting greyness, while this monotone,
Surly and distant, mixed inseparably
Into the clangour of the wind and sea.

" I hear my soul drop down into decay,
And Mananan's dark tower, stone after stone,
Gather sea slime and fall the seaward way,
And the moon goad the waters night and day,
That all be overthrown.

" But till the moon has taken all, I wage
War on the mightiest men under the skies,
And they have fallen or fled, age after age.
Light is man's love, and lighter is man's rage ;
His purpose drifts and dies."

And then lost Niam murmured, " Love, we go
To the Island of Forgetfulness, for lo !
The Islands of Dancing and of Victories
Are empty of all power."

           " And which of these
Is the Island of Content ? "

           " None know," she said ;
And on my bosom laid her weeping head.

BOOK III

FLED foam underneath us, and round us, a wandering
    and milky smoke,
High as the saddle girth, covering away from our
    glances the tide ;
And those that fled, and that followed, from the
    foam-pale distance broke ;
The immortal desire of immortals we saw in their
    faces, and sighed.

I mused on the chase with the Fenians, and Bran,
    Sgeolan, Lomair,
And never a song sang Niam, and over my finger-
    tips
Came now the sliding of tears and sweeping of mist-
    cold hair,
And now the warmth of sighs, and after the quiver
    of lips.

Were we days long or hours long in riding, when
    rolled in a grisly peace,
An isle lay level before us, with dripping hazel and
    oak ?
And we stood on a sea's edge we saw not ; for whiter
    than new-washed fleece
Fled foam underneath us, and round us, a wandering
    and milky smoke.

And we rode on the plains of the sea's edge ; the
    sea's edge barren and grey,
Grey sand on the green of the grasses and over the
    dripping trees,

Dripping and doubling landward, as though they
would hasten away
Like an army of old men longing for rest from the
moan of the seas.

But the trees grew taller and closer, immense in their
wrinkling bark ;
Dropping ; a murmurous dropping ; old silence
and that one sound ;
For no live creatures lived there, no weasels moved
in the dark :
Long sighs arose in our spirits, beneath us bubbled
the ground.

And the ears of the horse went sinking away in the
hollow night,
For, as drift from a sailor slow drowning the gleams
of the world and the sun,
Ceased on our hands and our faces, on hazel and oak
leaf, the light,
And the stars were blotted above us, and the whole
of the world was one.

Till the horse gave a whinny ; for, cumbrous with
stems of the hazel and oak,
A valley flowed down from his hoofs, and there in
the long grass lay,
Under the starlight and shadow, a monstrous
slumbering folk,
Their naked and gleaming bodies poured out and
heaped in the way.

And by them were arrow and war-axe, arrow and
    shield and blade ;
And dew-blanched horns, in whose hollow a child
    of three years old
Could sleep on a couch of rushes, and all inwrought
    and inlaid,
And more comely than man can make them with
    bronze and silver and gold.

And each of the huge white creatures was huger
    than fourscore men ;
The tops of their ears were feathered, their hands
    were the claws of birds,
And, shaking the plumes of the grasses and the
    leaves of the mural glen,
The breathing came from those bodies, long-warless,
    grown whiter than curds.

The wood was so spacious above them, that He who
    has stars for His flocks
Could fondle the leaves with His fingers, nor go from
    His dew-cumbered skies ;
So long were they sleeping, the owls had builded
    their nests in their locks,
Filling the fibrous dimness with long generations of
    eyes.

And over the limbs and the valley the slow owls
    wandered and came,
Now in a place of star-fire, and now in a shadow-
    place wide ;

And the chief of the huge white creatures, his knees
    in the soft star-flame,
Lay loose in a place of shadow : we drew the reins
    by his side.

Golden the nails of his bird-claws, flung loosely
    along the dim ground ;
In one was a branch soft-shining with bells more
    many than sighs
In midst of an old man's bosom ; owls ruffling and
    pacing around,
Sidled their bodies against him, filling the shade with
    their eyes.

And my gaze was thronged with the sleepers ; no,
    not since the world began,
In realms where the handsome were many, nor in
    glamours by demons flung,
Have faces alive with such beauty been known to the
    salt eye of man,
Yet weary with passions that faded when the seven-
    fold seas were young.

And I gazed on the bell-branch, sleep's forebear, far
    sung by the Sennachies.
I saw how those slumberers, grown weary, there
    camping in grasses deep,
Of wars with the wide world and pacing the shores
    of the wandering seas,
Laid hands on the bell-branch and swayed it, and fed
    of unhuman sleep.

Snatching the horn of Niam, I blew a long lingering
note.
Came sound from those monstrous sleepers, a sound
like the stirring of flies.
He, shaking the fold of his lips, and heaving the
pillar of his throat,
Watched me with mournful wonder out of the wells
of his eyes.

I cried, " Come out of the shadow, king of the nails
of gold !
And tell of your goodly household and the goodly
works of your hands,
That we may muse in the starlight and talk of the
battles of old ;
Your questioner, Usheen, is worthy, he comes from
the Fenian lands."

Half open his eyes were, and held me, dull with the
smoke of their dreams ;
His lips moved slowly in answer, no answer out of
them came ;
Then he swayed in his fingers the bell-branch, slow
dropping a sound in faint streams
Softer than snow-flakes in April and piercing the
marrow like flame.

Wrapt in the wave of that music, with weariness
more than of earth,
The moil of my centuries filled me ; and gone like a
sea-covered stone

Were the memories of the whole of my sorrow and
the memories of the whole of my mirth,
And a softness came from the starlight and filled me
full to the bone.

In the roots of the grasses, the sorrels, I laid my body
as low ;
And the pearl-pale Niam lay by me, her brow on the
midst of my breast ;
And the horse was gone in the distance, and years
after years 'gan flow ;
Square leaves of the ivy moved over us, binding us
down to our rest.

And, man of the many white croziers, a century there
I forgot ;
How the fetlocks drip blood in the battle, when the
fallen on fallen lie rolled ;
How the falconer follows the falcon in the weeds of
the heron's plot,
And the names of the demons whose hammers made
armour for Conhor of old.

And, man of the many white croziers, a century there
I forgot ;
That the spear-shaft is made out of ashwood, the
shield out of osier and hide ;
How the hammers spring on the anvil, on the spear-
head's burning spot ;
How the slow, blue-eyed oxen of Finn low sadly at
evening tide.

But in dreams, mild man of the croziers, driving the
    dust with their throngs,
Moved round me, of seamen or landsmen, all who
    are winter tales ;
Came by me the kings of the Red Branch, with roar-
    ing of laughter and songs,
Or moved as they moved once, love-making or
    piercing the tempest with sails.

Came Blanid, Mac Nessa, tall Fergus who feastward
    of old time slunk,
Cook Barach, the traitor ; and warward, the spittle
    on his beard never dry,
Dark Balor, as old as a forest, car-borne, his mighty
    head sunk
Helpless, men lifting the lids of his weary and death-
    making eye.

And by me, in soft red raiment, the Fenians moved
    in loud streams,
And Grania, walking and smiling, sewed with her
    needle of bone.
So lived I and lived not, so wrought I and wrought
    not, with creatures of dreams,
In a long iron sleep, as a fish in the water goes dumb
    as a stone.

At times our slumber was lightened.   When the sun
    was on silver or gold ;
When brushed with the wings of the owls, in the
    dimness they love going by ;

When a glow-worm was green on a grass leaf, lured
    from his lair in the mould ;
Half wakening, we lifted our eyelids, and gazed on
    the grass with a sigh.

So watched I when, man of the croziers, at the heel
    of a century fell,
Weak, in the midst of the meadow, from his miles in
    the midst of the air,
A starling like them that forgathered 'neath a moon
    waking white as a shell
When the Fenians made foray at morning with
    Bran, Sgeolan, Lomair.

I awoke : the strange horse without summons out of
    the distance ran,
Thrusting his nose to my shoulder ; he knew in his
    bosom deep
That once more moved in my bosom the ancient
    sadness of man,
And that I would leave the immortals, their dimness,
    their dews dropping sleep.

O, had you seen beautiful Niam grow white as the
    waters are white,
Lord of the croziers, you even had lifted your hands
    and wept :
But, the bird in my fingers, I mounted, remembering
    alone that delight
Of twilight and slumber were gone, and that hoofs
    impatiently stept.

I cried, " O Niam !   O white one ! if only a twelve-
        houred day,
I must gaze on the beard of Finn, and move where
        the old men and young
In the Fenians' dwellings of wattle lean on the chess-
        boards and play,
Ah, sweet to me now were even bald Conan's slander-
        ous tongue !

" Like me were some galley forsaken far off in
        Meridian isle,
Remembering its long-oared companions, sails
        turning to threadbare rags ;
No more to crawl on the seas with long oars mile
        after mile,
But to be amid shooting of flies and flowering of
        rushes and flags."

Their motionless eyeballs of spirits grown mild with
        mysterious thought,
Watched her those seamless faces from the valley's
        glimmering girth ;
As she murmured, " O wandering Usheen, the
        strength of the bell-branch is naught,
For there moves alive in your fingers the fluttering
        sadness of earth.

" Then go through the lands in the saddle and see
        what the mortals do,
And softly come to your Niam over the tops of the
        tide ;

But weep for your Niam, O Usheen, weep ; for if
  only your shoe
Brush lightly as haymouse earth's pebbles, you will
  come no more to my side.

" O flaming lion of the world, O when will you
  turn to your rest ? "
I saw from a distant saddle ; from the earth she
  made her moan ;
" I would die like a small withered leaf in the autumn,
  for breast unto breast
We shall mingle no more, nor our gazes empty their
  sweetness lone

" In the isles of the farthest seas where only the
  spirits come.
Were the winds less soft than the breath of a pigeon
  who sleeps on her nest,
Nor lost in the star-fires and odours the sound of the
  sea's vague drum ?
O flaming lion of the world, O when will you turn
  to your rest ? "

The wailing grew distant ; I rode by the woods of
  the wrinkling bark,
Where ever is murmurous dropping, old silence and
  that one sound ;
For no live creatures live there, no weasels move in
  the dark ;
In a reverie forgetful of all things, over the bubbling
  ground.

And I rode by the plains of the sea's edge, where all
    is barren and grey,
Grey sands on the green of the grasses and over the
    dripping trees,
Dripping and doubling landward, as though they
    would hasten away,
Like an army of old men longing for rest from the
    moan of the seas.

And the winds made the sands on the sea's edge
    turning and turning go,
As my mind made the names of the Fenians. Far
    from the hazel and oak,
I rode away on the surges, where, high as the saddle
    bow,
Fled foam underneath me, and round me, a wandering
    and milky smoke.

Long fled the foam-flakes around me, the winds fled
    out of the vast,
Snatching the bird in secret ; nor knew I, embosomed
    apart,
When they froze the cloth on my body like armour
    riveted fast,
For Remembrance, lifting her leanness, keened in
    the gates of my heart.

Till fattening the winds of the morning, an odour
    of new-mown hay
Came, and my forehead fell low, and my tears like
    berries fell down ;

D   37

Later a sound came, half lost in the sound of a shore
    far away,
From the great grass-barnacle calling, and later the
    shore-weeds brown.

If I were as I once was, the strong hoofs crushing
    the sand and the shells,
Coming out of the sea as the dawn comes, a chaunt
    of love on my lips,
Not coughing, my head on my knees, and praying,
    and wroth with the bells,
I would leave no saint's head on his body from
    Rachlin to Bera of ships.

Making way from the kindling surges, I rode on a
    bridle-path
Much wondering to see upon all hands, of wattles
    and woodwork made,
Your bell-mounted churches, and guardless the
    sacred cairn and the rath,
And a small and a feeble populace stooping with
    mattock and spade,

Or weeding or ploughing with faces a-shining with
    much-toil wet ;
While in this place and that place, with bodies
    unglorious, their chieftains stood,
Awaiting in patience the straw-death, croziered one,
    caught in your net :
Went the laughter of scorn from my mouth like the
    roaring of wind in a wood.

And because I went by them so huge and so speedy
    with eyes so bright,
Came after the hard gaze of youth, or an old man
    lifted his head :
And I rode and I rode, and I cried out, " The
    Fenians hunt wolves in the night,
So sleep thee by daytime." A voice cried, " The
    Fenians a long time are dead."

A whitebeard stood hushed on the pathway, the
    flesh of his face as dried grass,
And in folds round his eyes and his mouth, he sad as
    a child without milk ;
And the dreams of the islands were gone, and I knew
    how men sorrow and pass,
And their hound, and their horse, and their love, and
    their eyes that glimmer like silk.

And wrapping my face in my hair, I murmured,
    " In old age they ceased " ;
And my tears were larger than berries, and I mur-
    mured, " Where white clouds lie spread
On Crevroe or broad Knockfefin, with many of old
    they feast
On the floors of the gods." He cried, " No, the
    gods a long time are dead."

And lonely and longing for Niam, I shivered and
    turned me about,
The heart in me longing to leap like a grasshopper
    into her heart ;

I turned and rode to the westward, and followed the
  sea's old shout
Till I saw where Maive lies sleeping till starlight and
  midnight part.

And there at the foot of the mountain, two carried a
  sack full of sand,
They bore it with staggering and sweating, but fell
  with their burden at length.
Leaning down from the gem-studded saddle, I flung
  it five yards with my hand,
With a sob for men waxing so weakly, a sob for the
  Fenian's old strength.

The rest you have heard of, O croziered man ; how,
  when divided the girth,
I fell on the path, and the horse went away like a
  summer fly ;
And my years three hundred fell on me, and I rose,
  and walked on the earth,
A creeping old man, full of sleep, with the spittle on
  his beard never dry.

How the men of the sand-sack showed me a church
  with its belfry in air ;
Sorry place, where for swing of the war-axe in my
  dim eyes the crozier gleams ;
What place have Caolte and Conan, and Bran,
  Sgeolan, Lomair ?
Speak, you too are old with your memories, an old
  man surrounded with dreams.

Where the flesh of the footsole clingeth on the
    burning stones is their place ;
Where the demons whip them with wires on the
    burning stones of wide Hell,
Watching the blessed ones move far off, and the
    smile on God's face,
Between them a gateway of brass, and the howl of
    the angels who fell.

USHEEN

Put the staff in my hands ; for I go to the Fenians,
    O cleric, to chaunt
The war-songs that roused them of old ; they will
    rise, making clouds with their breath,
Innumerable, singing, exultant ; the clay under-
    neath them shall pant,
And demons be broken in pieces, and trampled
    beneath them in death.

And demons afraid in their darkness ; deep horror
    of eyes and of wings,
Afraid their ears on the earth laid, shall listen and
    rise up and weep ;
Hearing the shaking of shields and the quiver of
    stretched bowstrings,
Hearing Hell loud with a murmur, as shouting and
    mocking we sweep.

We will tear out the flaming stones, and batter the
    gateway of brass
And enter, and none sayeth " No " when there enters
    the strongly armed guest ;

Make clean as a broom cleans, and march on as oxen
    move over young grass ;
Then feast, making converse of wars, and of old
    wounds, and turn to our rest.

S. PATRIC

On the flaming stones, without refuge, the limbs of
    the Fenians are tost ;
None war on the masters of Hell, who could break
    up the world in their rage ;
But kneel and wear out the flags and pray for your
    soul that is lost
Through the demon love of its youth and its godless
    and passionate age.

USHEEN

Ah, me ! to be shaken with coughing and broken
    with old age and pain,
Without laughter, a show unto children, alone with
    remembrance and fear ;
All emptied of purple hours as a beggar's cloak in
    the rain,
As a hay-cock out on the flood, or a wolf sucked
    under a weir.

It were sad to gaze on the blessed and no man I loved
    of old there ;
I throw down the chain of small stones ! when life
    in my body has ceased,
I will go to Caolte, and Conan, and Bran, Sgeolan,
    Lomair,
And dwell in the house of the Fenians, be they in
    flames or at feast.

FROM "CROSSWAYS"
(1889)

THE INDIAN UPON GOD

I PASSED along the water's edge below the humid
    trees,
My spirit rocked in evening light, the rushes round
    my knees,
My spirit rocked in sleep and sighs ; and saw the
    moorfowl pace
All dripping on a grassy slope, and saw them cease to
    chase
Each other round in circles, and heard the eldest
    speak :
Who holds the world between His bill and made us strong
    or weak
Is an undying moorfowl, and He lives beyond the sky.
The rains are from His dripping wing, the moonbeams
    from His eye.
I passed a little further on and heard a lotus talk :
Who made the world and ruleth it, He hangeth on a stalk,
For I am in His image made, and all this tinkling tide
Is but a sliding drop of rain between His petals wide.
A little way within the gloom a roebuck raised his
    eyes
Brimful of starlight, and he said : *The Stamper of the*
    Skies,
He is a gentle roebuck ; for how else, I pray, could He
Conceive a thing so sad and soft, a gentle thing like me ?
I passed a little further on and heard a peacock say :
Who made the grass and made the worms and made my
    feathers gay,
He is a monstrous peacock, and He waveth all the night
His languid tail above us, lit with myriad spots of light.

THE STOLEN CHILD

WHERE dips the rocky highland
Of Sleuth Wood in the lake,
There lies a leafy island
Where flapping herons wake
The drowsy water rats ;
There we've hid our faery vats,
Full of berries,
And of reddest stolen cherries.
Come away, O human child !
To the waters and the wild
With a faery, hand in hand,
For the world's more full of weeping than you can under-
stand.

Where the wave of moonlight glosses
The dim grey sands with light,
Far off by furthest Rosses
We foot it all the night,
Weaving olden dances,
Mingling hands and mingling glances
Till the moon has taken flight ;
To and fro we leap
And chase the frothy bubbles,
While the world is full of troubles
And is anxious in its sleep.
Come away, O human child !
To the waters and the wild
With a faery, hand in hand,
For the world's more full of weeping than you can under-
stand.

Where the wandering water gushes
From the hills above Glen-Car,
In pools among the rushes
That scarce could bathe a star,
We seek for slumbering trout
And whispering in their ears
Give them unquiet dreams ;
Leaning softly out
From ferns that drop their tears
Over the young streams.
Come away, O human child !
To the waters and the wild
With a faery, hand in hand,
For the world's more full of weeping than you can under-
*   stand.*

Away with us he's going,
The solemn-eyed :
He'll hear no more the lowing
Of the calves on the warm hillside
Or the kettle on the hob
Sing peace into his breast,
Or see the brown mice bob
Round and round the oatmeal-chest.
For he comes, the human child,
To the waters and the wild
With a faery, hand in hand,
From a world more full of weeping than he can understand.

TO AN ISLE IN THE WATER

SHY one, shy one,
Shy one of my heart,
She moves in the firelight
Pensively apart.

She carries in the dishes,
And lays them in a row.
To an isle in the water
With her would I go.

She carries in the candles,
And lights the curtained room,
Shy in the doorway
And shy in the gloom ;

And shy as a rabbit,
Helpful and shy.
To an isle in the water
With her would I fly.

DOWN BY THE SALLEY GARDENS

Down by the salley gardens my love and I did meet;
She passed the salley gardens with little snow-white
feet.
She bid me take love easy, as the leaves grow on the
tree;
But I, being young and foolish, with her would not
agree.

In a field by the river my love and I did stand,
And on my leaning shoulder she laid her snow-white
hand.
She bid me take life easy, as the grass grows on the
weirs;
But I was young and foolish, and now am full of
tears.

FROM "THE ROSE"
(1893)

THE ROSE OF THE WORLD

Who dreamed that beauty passes like a dream?
For these red lips, with all their mournful pride,
Mournful that no new wonder may betide,
Troy passed away in one high funeral gleam,
And Usna's children died.

We and the labouring world are passing by:
Amid men's souls, that waver and give place
Like the pale waters in their wintry race,
Under the passing stars, foam of the sky,
Lives on this lonely face.

Bow down, archangels, in your dim abode:
Before you were, or any hearts to beat,
Weary and kind one lingered by His seat;
He made the world to be a grassy road
Before her wandering feet.

A FAERY SONG

Sung by the people of faery over Diarmuid and Grania, in their bridal sleep under a Cromlech.

We who are old, old and gay,
O so old !
Thousands of years, thousands of years,
If all were told :

Give to these children, new from the world,
Silence and love ;
And the long dew-dropping hours of the night,
And the stars above :

Give to these children, new from the world,
Rest far from men.
Is anything better, anything better ?
Tell us it then :

Us who are old, old and gay,
O so old !
Thousands of years, thousands of years,
If all were told.

THE LAKE ISLE OF INNISFREE

I WILL arise and go now, and go to Innisfree,
And a small cabin build there, of clay and wattles
    made :
Nine bean rows will I have there, a hive for the
    honey bee,
And live alone in the bee-loud glade.

And I shall have some peace there, for peace comes
    dropping slow,
Dropping from the veils of the morning to where
    the cricket sings ;
There midnight's all a glimmer, and noon a purple
    glow,
And evening full of the linnet's wings.

I will arise and go now, for always night and day
I hear lake water lapping with low sounds by the
    shore ;
While I stand on the roadway, or on the pavements
    grey,
I hear it in the deep heart's core.

A CRADLE SONG

The angels are stooping
Above your bed;
They weary of trooping
With the whimpering dead.

God's laughing in Heaven
To see you so good;
The Sailing Seven
Are gay with His mood.

I sigh that kiss you,
For I must own
That I shall miss you
When you have grown.

THE SORROW OF LOVE

THE brawling of a sparrow in the eaves,
The brilliant moon and all the milky sky,
And all that famous harmony of leaves,
Had blotted out man's image and his cry.

A girl arose that had red mournful lips
And seemed the greatness of the world in tears,
Doomed like Odysseus and the labouring ships
And proud as Priam murdered with his peers ;

Arose, and on the instant clamorous eaves,
A climbing moon upon an empty sky,
And all that lamentation of the leaves,
Could but compose man's image and his cry.

WHEN YOU ARE OLD

WHEN you are old and grey and full of sleep,
And nodding by the fire, take down this book,
And slowly read, and dream of the soft look
Your eyes had once, and of their shadows deep;

How many loved your moments of glad grace,
And loved your beauty with love false or true;
But one man loved the pilgrim soul in you,
And loved the sorrows of your changing face.

And bending down beside the glowing bars,
Murmur, a little sadly, how love fled
And paced upon the mountains overhead
And hid his face amid a crowd of stars.

THE MAN WHO DREAMED OF FAERYLAND

He stood among a crowd at Drumahair;
His heart hung all upon a silken dress,
And he had known at last some tenderness,
Before earth took him to her stony care;
But when a man poured fish into a pile,
It seemed they raised their little silver heads,
And sang what gold morning or evening sheds
Upon a woven world-forgotten isle
Where people love beside the ravelled seas;
That Time can never mar a lover's vows
Under that woven changeless roof of boughs:
The singing shook him out of his new ease.

He wandered by the sands of Lissadell;
His mind ran all on money cares and fears,
And he had known at last some prudent years
Before they heaped his grave under the hill;
But while he passed before a plashy place,
A lug-worm with its grey and muddy mouth
Sang that somewhere to north or west or south
There dwelt a gay, exulting, gentle race
Under the golden or the silver skies;
That if a dancer stayed his hungry foot
It seemed the sun and moon were in the fruit:
And at that singing he was no more wise.

He mused beside the well of Scanavin,
He mused upon his mockers: without fail
His sudden vengeance were a country tale,

When earthy night had drunk his body in;
But one small knot-grass growing by the pool
Sang where—unnecessary cruel voice—
Old silence bids its chosen race rejoice,
Whatever ravelled waters rise and fall
Or stormy silver fret the gold of day,
And midnight there enfold them like a fleece
And lover there by lover be at peace.
The tale drove his fine angry mood away.

He slept under the hill of Lugnagall;
And might have known at last unhaunted sleep
Under that cold and vapour-turbaned steep,
Now that the earth had taken man and all:
Did not the worms that spired about his bones
Proclaim with that unwearied, reedy cry
That God has laid His fingers on the sky,
That from those fingers glittering summer runs
Upon the dancer by the dreamless wave.
Why should those lovers that no lovers miss
Dream, until God burn Nature with a kiss?
The man has found no comfort in the grave.

THE TWO TREES

Beloved, gaze in thine own heart,
The holy tree is growing there ;
From joy the holy branches start,
And all the trembling flowers they bear.
The changing colours of its fruit
Have dowered the stars with merry light ;
The surety of its hidden root
Has planted quiet in the night ;
The shaking of its leafy head
Has given the waves their melody,
And made my lips and music wed,
Murmuring a wizard song for thee.
There the Loves—a circle—go,
The flaming circle of our days,
Gyring, spiring to and fro
In those great ignorant leafy ways ;
Remembering all that shaken hair
And how the wingèd sandals dart,
Thine eyes grow full of tender care :
Beloved, gaze in thine own heart.

Gaze no more in the bitter glass
The demons, with their subtle guile,
Lift up before us when they pass,
Or only gaze a little while ;
For there a fatal image grows
That the stormy night receives,
Roots half hidden under snows,
Broken boughs and blackened leaves.
For all things turn to barrenness
In the dim glass the demons hold,

The glass of outer weariness,
Made when God slept in times of old.
There, through the broken branches, go
The ravens of unresting thought ;
Flying, crying to and fro,
Cruel claw and hungry throat,
Or else they stand and sniff the wind,
And shake their ragged wings ; alas !
Thy tender eyes grow all unkind :
Gaze no more in the bitter glass.

TO IRELAND IN THE COMING TIMES

KNOW, that I would accounted be
True brother of that company,
Who sang to sweeten Ireland's wrong,
Ballad and story, rann and song;
Nor be I any less of them,
Because the red-rose-bordered hem
Of her, whose history began
Before God made the angelic clan,
Trails all about the written page.
When Time began to rant and rage
The measure of her flying feet
Made Ireland's heart begin to beat;
And Time bade all his candles flare
To light a measure here and there;
And may the thoughts of Ireland brood
Upon a measured quietude.

Nor may I less be counted one
With Davis, Mangan, Ferguson,
Because to him, who ponders well,
My rhymes more than their rhyming tell
Of things discovered in the deep,
Where only body's laid asleep.
For the elemental creatures go
About my table to and fro,
That hurry from unmeasured mind
To rant and rage in flood and wind;
Yet he who treads in measured ways
May surely barter gaze for gaze.
Man ever journeys on with them
After the red-rose-bordered hem.

Ah, faeries, dancing under the moon,
A Druid land, a Druid tune !

While still I may, I write for you
The love I lived, the dream I knew.
From our birthday, until we die,
Is but the winking of an eye ;
And we, our singing and our love,
What measurer Time has lit above,
And all benighted things that go
About my table to and fro,
Are passing on to where may be,
In truth's consuming ecstasy,
No place for love and dream at all ;
For God goes by with white foot-fall.
I cast my heart into my rhymes,
That you, in the dim coming times,
May know how my heart went with them
After the red-rose-bordered hem.

FROM
"THE WIND AMONG THE REEDS"
(1899)

THE host is riding from Knocknarea
And over the grave of Clooth-na-bare;
Caolte tossing his burning hair
And Niam calling *Away, come away:*
Empty your heart of its mortal dream.
The winds awaken, the leaves whirl round,
Our cheeks are pale, our hair is unbound,
Our breasts are heaving, our eyes are agleam,
Our arms are waving, our lips are apart;
And if any gaze on our rushing band,
We come between him and the deed of his hand,
We come between him and the hope of his heart.
The host is rushing 'twixt night and day,
And where is there hope or deed as fair?
Caolte tossing his burning hair,
And Niam calling *Away, come away.*

THE EVERLASTING VOICES

O SWEET everlasting Voices, be still;
Go to the guards of the heavenly fold
And bid them wander obeying your will,
Flame under flame, till Time be no more;
Have you not heard that our hearts are old,
That you call in birds, in wind on the hill,
In shaken boughs, in tide on the shore?
O sweet everlasting Voices, be still.

THE UNAPPEASABLE HOST

THE Danaan children laugh, in cradles of wrought
    gold,
And clap their hands together, and half close their
    eyes,
For they will ride the North when the ger-eagle flies,
With heavy whitening wings, and a heart fallen cold :
I kiss my wailing child and press it to my breast,
And hear the narrow graves calling my child and me.
Desolate winds that cry over the wandering sea ;
Desolate winds that hover in the flaming West ;
Desolate winds that beat the doors of Heaven, and
    beat
The doors of Hell and blow there many a whimper-
    ing ghost ;
O heart the winds have shaken ; the unappeasable
    host
Is comelier than candles at Mother Mary's feet.

INTO THE TWILIGHT

Out-worn heart, in a time out-worn,
Come clear of the nets of wrong and right;
Laugh, heart, again in the grey twilight,
Sigh, heart, again in the dew of the morn.

Your mother Eire is always young,
Dew ever shining and twilight grey;
Though hope fall from you and love decay,
Burning in fires of a slanderous tongue.

Come, heart, where hill is heaped upon hill:
For there the mystical brotherhood
Of sun and moon and hollow and wood
And river and stream work out their will;

And God stands winding His lonely horn,
And time and the world are ever in flight;
And love is less kind than the grey twilight,
And hope is less dear than the dew of the morn.

THE SONG OF WANDERING AENGUS

I WENT out to the hazel wood,
Because a fire was in my head,
And cut and peeled a hazel wand,
And hooked a berry to a thread;
And when white moths were on the wing,
And moth-like stars were flickering out,
I dropped the berry in a stream
And caught a little silver trout.

When I had laid it on the floor
I went to blow the fire aflame,
But something rustled on the floor,
And some one called me by my name:
It had become a glimmering girl
With apple blossom in her hair
Who called me by my name and ran
And faded through the brightening air.

Though I am old with wandering
Through hollow lands and hilly lands,
I will find out where she has gone,
And kiss her lips and take her hands;
And walk among long dappled grass,
And pluck till time and times are done
The silver apples of the moon,
The golden apples of the sun.

I RISE in the dawn, and I kneel and blow
Till the seed of the fire flicker and glow;
And then I must scrub and bake and sweep
Till stars are beginning to blink and peep;
And the young lie long and dream in their bed
Of the matching of ribbons for bosom and head,
And their day goes over in idleness,
And they sigh if the wind but lift a tress:
While I must work because I am old,
And the seed of the fire gets feeble and cold.

HE BIDS HIS BELOVED BE AT PEACE

I HEAR the Shadowy Horses, their long manes
    a-shake,
Their hoofs heavy with tumult, their eyes glimmering
    white ;
The North unfolds above them clinging, creeping
    night,
The East her hidden joy before the morning break,
The West weeps in pale dew and sighs passing away,
The South is pouring down roses of crimson fire :
O vanity of Sleep, Hope, Dream, endless Desire,
The Horses of Disaster plunge in the heavy clay :
Beloved, let your eyes half close, and your heart beat
Over my heart, and your hair fall over my breast,
Drowning love's lonely hour in deep twilight of rest,
And hiding their tossing manes and their tumultuous
    feet.

O, CURLEW, cry no more in the air,
Or only to the water in the West ;
Because your crying brings to my mind
Passion-dimmed eyes and long heavy hair
That was shaken out over my breast :
There is enough evil in the crying of wind.

WHEN my arms wrap you round I press
My heart upon the loveliness
That has long faded from the world;
The jewelled crowns that kings have hurled
In shadowy pools, when armies fled;
The love-tales wrought with silken thread
By dreaming ladies upon cloth
That has made fat the murderous moth;
The roses that of old time were
Woven by ladies in their hair,
The dew-cold lilies ladies bore
Through many a sacred corridor
Where such grey clouds of incense rose
That only God's eyes did not close:
For that pale breast and lingering hand
Come from a more dream-heavy land,
A more dream-heavy hour than this;
And when you sigh from kiss to kiss
I hear white Beauty sighing, too,
For hours when all must fade like dew,
But flame on flame, and deep on deep,
Throne over throne where in half sleep,
Their swords upon their iron knees,
Brood her high lonely mysteries.

TO HIS HEART, BIDDING IT HAVE NO FEAR

BE you still, be you still, trembling heart;
Remember the wisdom out of the old days:
Him who trembles before the flame and the flood,
And the winds that blow through the starry ways,
Let the starry winds and the flame and the flood
Cover over and hide, for he has no part
With the lonely, majestical multitude.

THE CAP AND BELLS

THE jester walked in the garden :
The garden had fallen still ;
He bade his soul rise upward
And stand on her window-sill.

It rose in a straight blue garment,
When owls began to call :
It had grown wise-tongued by thinking
Of a quiet and light footfall ;

But the young queen would not listen ;
She rose in her pale night-gown ;
She drew in the heavy casement
And pushed the latches down.

He bade his heart go to her,
When the owls called out no more ;
In a red and quivering garment
It sang to her through the door.

It had grown sweet-tongued by dreaming
Of a flutter of flower-like hair ;
But she took up her fan from the table
And waved it off on the air.

" I have cap and bells," he pondered,
" I will send them to her and die " ;
And when the morning whitened
He left them where she went by.

She laid them upon her bosom,
Under a cloud of her hair,
And her red lips sang them a love-song:
Till stars grew out of the air.

She opened her door and her window,
And the heart and the soul came through,
To her right hand came the red one,
To her left hand came the blue.

They set up a noise like crickets,
A chattering wise and sweet,
And her hair was a folded flower
And the quiet of love in her feet.

THE LOVER PLEADS WITH HIS FRIEND FOR
OLD FRIENDS

Though you are in your shining days,
Voices among the crowd
And new friends busy with your praise,
Be not unkind or proud,
But think about old friends the most:
Time's bitter flood will rise,
Your beauty perish and be lost
For all eyes but these eyes.

HE WISHES FOR THE CLOTHS OF HEAVEN

HAD I the heavens' embroidered cloths,
Enwrought with golden and silver light,
The blue and the dim and the dark cloths
Of night and light and the half light,
I would spread the cloths under your feet :
But I, being poor, have only my dreams ;
I have spread my dreams under your feet ;
Tread softly because you tread on my dreams.

THE FIDDLER OF DOONEY

WHEN I play on my fiddle in Dooney,
Folk dance like a wave of the sea ;
My cousin is priest in Kilvarnet,
My brother in Mocharabuiee.

I passed my brother and cousin :
They read in their books of prayer ;
I read in my book of songs
I bought at the Sligo fair.

When we come at the end of time,
To Peter sitting in state,
He will smile on the three old spirits,
But call me first through the gate ;

For the good are always the merry,
Save by an evil chance,
And the merry love the fiddle
And the merry love to dance :

And when the folk there spy me,
They will all come up to me,
With " Here is the fiddler of Dooney ! "
And dance like a wave of the sea.

BAILE AND AILLINN

(1903)

Argument. Baile and Aillinn were lovers, but Aengus, the Master of Love, wishing them to be happy in his own land among the dead, told to each a story of the other's death, so that their hearts were broken and they died.

I HARDLY hear the curlew cry,
Nor the grey rush when the wind is high,
Before my thoughts begin to run
On the heir of Ulad, Buan's son,
Baile, who had the honey mouth ;
And that mild woman of the south,
Aillinn, who was King Lugaid's heir.
Their love was never drowned in care
Of this or that thing, nor grew cold
Because their bodies had grown old.
Being forbid to marry on earth,
They blossomed to immortal mirth.

About the time when Christ was born,
When the long wars for the White Horn
And the Brown Bull had not yet come,
Young Baile Honey-Mouth, whom some
Called rather Baile Little-Land,
Rode out of Emain with a band
Of harpers and young men ; and they
Imagined, as they struck the way
To many-pastured Muirthemne,
That all things fell out happily,
And there, for all that fools had said,
Baile and Aillinn would be wed.

They found an old man running there :
He had ragged long grass-coloured hair ;

He had knees that stuck out of his hose ;
He had puddle water in his shoes ;
He had half a cloak to keep him dry,
Although he had a squirrel's eye.

O wandering birds and rushy beds,
You put such folly in our heads
With all this crying in the wind ,
No common love is to our mind,
And our poor Kate or Nan is less
Than any whose unhappiness
Awoke the harp-strings long ago.
Yet they that know all things but know
That all this life can give us is
A child's laughter, a woman's kiss.
Who was it put so great a scorn
In the grey reeds that night and morn
Are trodden and broken by the herds,
And in the light bodies of birds
That north wind tumbles to and fro
And pinches among hail and snow ?

That runner said : " I am from the south ;
I run to Baile Honey-Mouth,
To tell him how the girl Aillinn
Rode from the country of her kin,
And old and young men rode with her :
For all that country had been astir
If anybody half as fair
Had chosen a husband anywhere
But where it could see her every day.
When they had ridden a little way

An old man caught the horse's head
With : ' You must home again, and wed
With somebody in your own land.'
A young man cried and kissed her hand,
' O lady, wed with one of us ' ;
And when no face grew piteous
For any gentle thing she spake,
She fell and died of the heart-break."

Because a lover's heart's worn out,
Being tumbled and blown about
By its own blind imagining,
And will believe that anything
That is bad enough to be true, is true,
Baile's heart was broken in two ;
And he, being laid upon green boughs,
Was carried to the goodly house
Where the Hound of Ulad sat before
The brazen pillars of his door,
His face bowed low to weep the end
Of the harper's daughter and her friend.
For although years had passed away
He always wept them on that day,
For on that day they had been betrayed ;
And now that Honey-Mouth is laid
Under a cairn of sleepy stone
Before his eyes, he has tears for none,
Although he is carrying stone, but two
For whom the cairn's but heaped anew.

We hold because our memory is
So full of that thing and of this

That out of sight is out of mind.
But the grey rush under the wind
And the grey bird with crooked bill
Have such long memories, that they still
Remember Deirdre and her man ;
And when we walk with Kate or Nan
About the windy water side,
Our hearts can hear the voices chide.
How could we be so soon content,
Who know the way that Naoise went ?
And they have news of Deirdre's eyes,
Who being lovely was so wise—
Ah ! wise, my heart knows well how wise.

Now had that old gaunt crafty one,
Gathering his cloak about him, run
Where Aillinn rode with waiting maids,
Who amid leafy lights and shades
Dreamed of the hands that would unlace
Their bodices in some dim place
When they had come to the marriage bed ;
And harpers, pacing with high head
As though their music were enough
To make the savage heart of love
Grow gentle without sorrowing,
Imagining and pondering
Heaven knows what calamity ;

" Another's hurried off," cried he,
" From heat and cold and wind and wave ;
They have heaped the stones above his grave
In Muirthemne, and over it
In changeless Ogham letters writ—

Baile, that was of Rury's seed.
But the gods long ago decreed
No waiting maid should ever spread
Baile and Aillinn's marriage bed,
For they should clip and clip again
Where wild bees hive on the Great Plain.
Therefore it is but little news
That put this hurry in my shoes."

Then seeing that he scarce had spoke
Before her love-worn heart had broke,
He ran and laughed until he came
To that high hill the herdsmen name
The Hill Seat of Leighin, because
Some god or king had made the laws
That held the land together there,
In old times among the clouds of the air.

That old man climbed ; the day grew dim ;
Two swans came flying up to him,
Linked by a gold chain each to each,
And with low murmuring laughing speech
Alighted on the windy grass.
They knew him : his changed body was
Tall, proud and ruddy, and light wings
Were hovering over the harp-strings
That Etain, Midhir's wife, had wove
In the hid place, being crazed by love.

What shall I call them ? fish that swim,
Scale rubbing scale where light is dim
By a broad water-lily leaf ;
Or mice in the one wheaten sheaf

Forgotten at the threshing place;
Or birds lost in the one clear space
Of morning light in a dim sky;
Or, it may be, the eyelids of one eye,
Or the door pillars of one house,
Or two sweet blossoming apple-boughs
That have one shadow on the ground;
Or the two strings that made one sound
Where that wise harper's finger ran.
For this young girl and this young man
Have happiness without an end,
Because they have made so good a friend.

They know all wonders, for they pass
The towery gates of Gorias,
And Findrias and Falias,
And long-forgotten Murias,
Among the giant kings whose hoard,
Cauldron and spear and stone and sword,
Was robbed before earth gave the wheat;
Wandering from broken street to street
They come where some huge watcher is,
And tremble with their love and kiss.

They know undying things, for they
Wander where earth withers away,
Though nothing troubles the great streams
But light from the pale stars, and gleams
From the holy orchards, where there is none
But fruit that is of precious stone,
Or apples of the sun and moon.

What were our praise to them ? They eat
Quiet's wild heart, like daily meat ;
Who when night thickens are afloat
On dappled skins in a glass boat,
Far out under a windless sky ;
While over them birds of Aengus fly,
And over the tiller and the prow,
And waving white wings to and fro
Awaken wanderings of light air
To stir their coverlet and their hair.

And poets found, old writers say,
A yew tree where his body lay ;
But a wild apple hid the grass
With its sweet blossom where hers was ;
And being in good heart, because
A better time had come again
After the deaths of many men,
And that long fighting at the ford,
They wrote on tablets of thin board,
Made of the apple and the yew,
All the love stories that they knew.

Let rush and bird cry out their fill
Of the harper's daughter if they will,
Beloved, I am not afraid of her.
She is not wiser nor lovelier,
And you are more high of heart than she,
For all her wanderings over-sea ;
But I'd have bird and rush forget
Those other two ; for never yet
Has lover lived, but longed to wive
Like them that are no more alive.

FROM
"IN THE SEVEN WOODS"
(1904)

THE FOLLY OF BEING COMFORTED

ONE that is ever kind said yesterday :
" Your well-belovèd's hair has threads of grey,
And little shadows come about her eyes ;
Time can but make it easier to be wise
Though now it seem impossible, and so
All that you need is patience."

                         Heart cries "No.
I have not a crumb of comfort, not a grain,
Time can but make her beauty over again :
Because of that great nobleness of hers
The fire that stirs about her, when she stirs
Burns but more clearly. O she had not these ways,
When all the wild summer was in her gaze."

O heart ! O heart ! if she'd but turn her head,
You'd know the folly of being comforted.

I CRIED when the moon was murmuring to the birds :
" Let peewit call and curlew cry where they will,
I long for your merry and tender and pitiful words,
For the roads are unending, and there is no place to
　　my mind."
The honey-pale moon lay low on the sleepy hill,
And I fell asleep upon lonely Echtge of streams.
No boughs have withered because of the wintry
　　wind ;
The boughs have withered because I have told them
　　my dreams.

I know of the leafy paths that the witches take,
Who come with their crowns of pearl and their
　　spindles of wool,
And their secret smile, out of the depths of the lake ;
I know where a dim moon drifts, where the Danaan
　　kind
Wind and unwind their dances when the light grows
　　cool
On the island lawns, their feet where the pale foam
　　gleams.
No boughs have withered because of the wintry
　　wind ;
The boughs have withered because I have told them
　　my dreams.

I know of the sleepy country, where swans fly round
Coupled with golden chains, and sing as they fly.
A king and a queen are wandering there, and the
　　sound

Has made them so happy and hopeless, so deaf and
    so blind
With wisdom, they wander till all the years have
    gone by ;
I know, and the curlew and peewit on Echtge of
    streams.
No boughs have withered because of the wintry
    wind ;
The boughs have withered because I have told them
    my dreams.

The old brown thorn trees break in two high over
    Cummen Strand,
Under a bitter black wind that blows from the left
    hand ;
Our courage breaks like an old tree in a black wind
    and dies,
But we have hidden in our hearts the flame out of
    the eyes
Of Cathleen, the daughter of Houlihan.

The wind has bundled up the clouds high over
    Knocknarea,
And thrown the thunder on the stones for all that
    Maeve can say.
Angers that are like noisy clouds have set our hearts
    abeat ;
But we have all bent low and low and kissed the
    quiet feet
Of Cathleen, the daughter of Houlihan.

The yellow pool has overflowed high up on Clooth-
    na-Bare,
For the wet winds are blowing out of the clinging air ;
Like heavy flooded waters our bodies and our blood ;
But purer than a tall candle before the Holy Rood
Is Cathleen, the daughter of Houlihan.

THE OLD MEN ADMIRING THEMSELVES
IN THE WATER

I HEARD the old, old men say,
" Everything alters,
And one by one we drop away."
They had hands like claws, and their knees
Were twisted like the old thorn trees
By the waters.
I heard the old, old men say,
" All that's beautiful drifts away
Like the waters."

THE RAGGED WOOD

O HURRY where by water among the trees
The delicate stepping stag and his lady sigh,
When they have but looked upon their images—
Would none had ever loved but you and I!

Or have you heard that sliding silver-shoed
Pale silver-proud queen-woman of the sky,
When the sun looked out of his golden hood?—
O that none ever loved but you and I!

O hurry to the ragged wood, for there
I will drive all those lovers out and cry—
O my share of the world, O yellow hair!
No one has ever loved but you and I.

THE HAPPY TOWNLAND

THERE'S many a strong farmer
Whose heart would break in two,
If he could see the townland
That we are riding to ;
Boughs have their fruit and blossom
At all times of the year ;
Rivers are running over
With red beer and brown beer.
An old man plays the bagpipes
In a golden and silver wood ;
Queens, their eyes blue like the ice,
Are dancing in a crowd.

The little fox he murmured,
" O what of the world's bane ? "
The sun was laughing sweetly,
The moon plucked at my rein ;
But the little red fox murmured,
" O do not pluck at his rein,
He is riding to the townland
That is the world's bane."

When their hearts are so high
That they would come to blows,
They unhook their heavy swords
From golden and silver boughs ;
But all that are killed in battle
Awaken to life again.
It is lucky that their story
Is not known among men,
For O, the strong farmers

That would let the spade lie,
Their hearts would be like a cup
That somebody had drunk dry.

The little fox he murmured,
" O what of the world's bane ? "
The sun was laughing sweetly,
The moon plucked at my rein ;
But the little red fox murmured,
" O do not pluck at his rein,
He is riding to the townland
That is the world's bane."

Michael will unhook his trumpet
From a bough overhead,
And blow a little noise
When the supper has been spread.
Gabriel will come from the water
With a fish tail, and talk
Of wonders that have happened
On wet roads where men walk,
And lift up an old horn
Of hammered silver, and drink
Till he has fallen asleep
Upon the starry brink.

The little fox he murmured,
" O what of the world's bane ? "
The sun was laughing sweetly,
The moon plucked at my rein ;
But the little red fox murmured,
" O do not pluck at his rein,
He is riding to the townland
That is the world's bane."

FROM "THE GREEN HELMET
AND OTHER POEMS"
(1912)

THE MASK

" Put off that mask of burning gold
With emerald eyes."
" O no, my dear, you make so bold
To find if hearts be wild and wise,
And yet not cold."

" I would but find what's there to find,
Love or deceit."
" It was the mask engaged your mind,
And after set your heart to beat,
Not what's behind."

" But lest you are my enemy,
I must enquire."
" O no, my dear, let all that be,
What matter, so there is but fire
In you, in me ? "

THESE ARE THE CLOUDS

THESE are the clouds about the fallen sun,
The majesty that shuts his burning eye :
The weak lay hand on what the strong has done,
Till that be tumbled that was lifted high
And discord follow upon unison,
And all things at one common level lie.
And therefore, friend, if your great race were run
And these things came, so much the more thereby
Have you made greatness your companion,
Although it be for children that you sigh :
These are the clouds about the fallen sun,
The majesty that shuts his burning eye.

FROM "RESPONSIBILITIES"

(1914)

PARDON, old fathers, if you still remain
Somewhere in ear-shot for the story's end,
Old Dublin merchant "free of ten and four"
Or trading out of Galway into Spain ;
Old country scholar, Robert Emmet's friend,
A hundred-year-old memory to the poor ;
Merchant and scholar who have left me blood
That has not passed through any huckster's loin,
Soldiers that gave, whatever die was cast :
A Butler or an Armstrong that withstood
Beside the brackish waters of the Boyne
James and his Irish when the Dutchman crossed ;
Old merchant skipper that leaped overboard
After a ragged hat in Biscay Bay,
You most of all, silent and fierce old man,
Because the daily spectacle that stirred
My fancy, and set my boyish lips to say
"Only the wasteful virtues earn the sun" ;
Pardon that for a barren passion's sake,
Although I have come close on forty-nine,
I have no child, I have nothing but a book,
Nothing but that to prove your blood and mine.

    January 1914.

POETS *with whom I learned my trade,*
Companions of the Cheshire Cheese,
Here's an old story I've re-made,
Imagining 'twould better please
Your ears than stories now in fashion,
Though you may think I waste my breath
Pretending that there can be passion
That has more life in it than death,
And though at bottling of your wine
Old wholesome Goban had no say ;
The moral's yours because it's mine.

When cups went round at close of day—
Is not that how good stories run ?—
The gods were sitting at the board
In their great house at Slievenamon.
They sang a drowsy song, or snored,
For all were full of wine and meat.
The smoky torches made a glare
On metal Goban 'd hammered at,
On old deep silver rolling there
Or on some still unemptied cup
That he, when frenzy stirred his thews,
Had hammered out on mountain top
To hold the sacred stuff he brews
That only gods may buy of him.

Now from that juice that made them wise
All those had lifted up the dim
Imaginations of their eyes,
For one that was like woman made

Before their sleepy eyelids ran
And trembling with her passion said,
" Come out and dig for a dead man,
Who's burrowing somewhere in the ground,
And mock him to his face and then
Hollo him on with horse and hound,
For he is the worst of all dead men."

We should be dazed and terror-struck,
If we but saw in dreams that room,
Those wine-drenched eyes, and curse our luck
That emptied all our days to come.
I knew a woman none could please,
Because she dreamed when but a child
Of men and women made like these ;
And after, when her blood ran wild,
Had ravelled her own story out,
And said, " In two or in three years
I needs must marry some poor lout,"
And having said it burst in tears.

Since, tavern comrades, you have died,
Maybe your images have stood,
Mere bone and muscle thrown aside,
Before that roomful or as good.
You had to face your ends when young—
'Twas wine or women, or some curse—
But never made a poorer song
That you might have a heavier purse,
Nor gave loud service to a cause
That you might have a troop of friends.
You kept the Muses' sterner laws,
And unrepenting faced your ends,

And therefore earned the right—and yet
Dowson and Johnson most I praise—
To troop with those the world's forgot,
And copy their proud steady gaze.

" The Danish troop was driven out
Between the dawn and dusk," she said ;
" Although the event was long in doubt,
Although the King of Ireland's dead
And half the kings, before sundown
All was accomplished.

     " When this day
Murrough, the King of Ireland's son,
Foot after foot was giving way,
He and his best troops back to back
Had perished there, but the Danes ran,
Stricken with panic from the attack,
The shouting of an unseen man ;
And being thankful Murrough found,
Led by a footsole dipped in blood
That had made prints upon the ground,
Where by old thorn trees that man stood ;
And though when he gazed here and there,
He had but gazed on thorn trees, spoke,
' Who is the friend that seems but air
And yet could give so fine a stroke ? '
Thereon a young man met his eye,
Who said, ' Because she held me in
Her love, and would not have me die,
Rock-nurtured Aoife took a pin,
And pushing it into my shirt,
Promised that for a pin's sake
No man should see to do me hurt ;

But there it's gone; I will not take
The fortune that had been my shame
Seeing, King's son, what wounds you have.'
'Twas roundly spoke, but when night came
He had betrayed me to his grave,
For he and the King's son were dead.
I'd promised him two hundred years,
And when for all I'd done or said—
And these immortal eyes shed tears—
He claimed his country's need was most,
I'd saved his life, yet for the sake
Of a new friend he has turned a ghost.
What does he care if my heart break?
I call for spade and horse and hound
That we may harry him."   Thereon
She cast herself upon the ground
And rent her clothes and made her moan:
" Why are they faithless when their might
Is from the holy shades that rove
The grey rock and the windy light?
Why should the faithfullest heart most love
The bitter sweetness of false faces?
Why must the lasting love what passes,
Why are the gods by men betrayed ! "

But thereon every god stood up
With a slow smile and without sound,
And stretching forth his arm and cup
To where she moaned upon the ground,
Suddenly drenched her to the skin;
And she with Goban's wine adrip,
No more remembering what had been,
Stared at the gods with laughing lip.

I have kept my faith, though faith was tried,
To that rock-born, rock-wandering foot,
And the world's altered since you died,
And I am in no good repute
With the loud host before the sea,
That think sword strokes were better meant
Than lover's music—let that be,
So that the wandering foot's content.

WHAT need you, being come to sense,
But fumble in a greasy till
And add the halfpence to the pence
And prayer to shivering prayer, until
You have dried the marrow from the bone?
For men were born to pray and save:
Romantic Ireland's dead and gone,
It's with O'Leary in the grave.

Yet they were of a different kind,
The names that stilled your childish play,
They have gone about the world like wind,
But little time had they to pray
For whom the hangman's rope was spun,
And what, God help us, could they save?
Romantic Ireland's dead and gone,
It's with O'Leary in the grave.

Was it for this the wild geese spread
The grey wing upon every tide;
For this that all that blood was shed,
For this Edward Fitzgerald died,
And Robert Emmet and Wolfe Tone,
All that delirium of the brave?
Romantic Ireland's dead and gone,
It's with O'Leary in the grave.

Yet could we turn the years again,
And call those exiles as they were
In all their loneliness and pain,
You'd cry " Some woman's yellow hair

Has maddened every mother's son " :
They weighed so lightly what they gave,
But let them be, they're dead and gone,
They're with O'Leary in the grave.

TO A FRIEND WHOSE WORK HAS COME
TO NOTHING

Now all the truth is out,
Be secret and take defeat
From any brazen throat,
For how can you compete,
Being honour bred, with one
Who, were it proved he lies,
Were neither shamed in his own
Nor in his neighbours' eyes ?
Bred to a harder thing
Than Triumph, turn away
And like a laughing string
Whereon mad fingers play
Amid a place of stone,
Be secret and exult,
Because of all things known
That is most difficult.

TO A SHADE

If you have revisited the town, thin Shade,
Whether to look upon your monument
(I wonder if the builder has been paid)
Or happier-thoughted when the day is spent
To drink of that salt breath out of the sea
When grey gulls flit about instead of men,
And the gaunt houses put on majesty :
Let these content you and be gone again ;
For they are at their old tricks yet.

         A man
Of your own passionate serving kind who had
  brought
In his full hands what, had they only known,
Had given their children's children loftier thought,
Sweeter emotion, working in their veins
Like gentle blood, has been driven from the place,
And insult heaped upon him for his pains
And for his open-handedness, disgrace ;
Your enemy, an old foul mouth, had set
The pack upon him.

       Go, unquiet wanderer,
And gather the Glasnevin coverlet
About your head till the dust stops your ear,
The time for you to taste of that salt breath
And listen at the corners has not come ;
You had enough of sorrow before death—
Away, away ! You are safer in the tomb.

September 29, 1913.

WHEN HELEN LIVED

WE have cried in our despair
That men desert,
For some trivial affair
Or noisy, insolent, sport,
Beauty that we have won
From bitterest hours ;
Yet we, had we walked within
Those topless towers
Where Helen walked with her boy,
Had given but as the rest
Of the men and women of Troy,
A word and a jest.

RUNNING TO PARADISE

As I came over Windy Gap
They threw a halfpenny into my cap,
For I am running to Paradise ;
And all that I need do is to wish
And somebody puts his hand in the dish
To throw me a bit of salted fish :
And there the king *is* but as the beggar.

My brother Mourteen is worn out
With skelping his big brawling lout,
And I am running to Paradise ;
A poor life, do what he can,
And though he keep a dog and a gun,
A serving maid and a serving man :
And there the king *is* but as the beggar.

Poor men have grown to be rich men,
And rich men grown to be poor again,
And I am running to Paradise ;
And many a darling wit's grown dull
That tossed a bare heel when at school,
Now it has filled an old sock full :
And there the king *is* but as the beggar.

The wind is old and still at play
While I must hurry upon my way,
For I am running to Paradise ;
Yet never have I lit on a friend
To take my fancy like the wind
That nobody can buy or bind :
And there the king *is* but as the beggar.

THE HOUR BEFORE DAWN

A CURSING rogue with a merry face,
A bundle of rags upon a crutch,
Stumbled upon that windy place
Called Croghan, and it was as much
As the one sturdy leg could do
To keep him upright while he cursed.
He had counted, where long years ago
Queen Maeve's nine Maines had been nursed,
A pair of lapwings, one old sheep
And not a house to the plain's edge,
When close to his right hand a heap
Of grey stones and a rocky ledge
Reminded him that he could make,
If he but shifted a few stones,
A shelter till the daylight broke.

But while he fumbled with the stones
They toppled over ; " Were it not
I have a lucky wooden shin
I had been hurt " ; and toppling brought
Before his eyes, where stones had been,
A dark deep hollow in the rock.
He gave a gasp and thought to have fled,
Being certain it was no right rock
Because an ancient history said
Hell Mouth lay open near that place,
And yet stood still, because inside
A great lad with a beery face
Had tucked himself away beside
A ladle and a tub of beer,
And snored, no phantom by his look.

So with a laugh at his own fear
He crawled into that pleasant nook.

" Night grows uneasy near the dawn
Till even I sleep light ; but who
Has tired of his own company ?
What one of Maeve's nine brawling sons
Sick of his grave has wakened me ?
But let him keep his grave for once
That I may find the sleep I have lost."

" What care I if you sleep or wake ?
But I'll have no man call me ghost."

" Say what you please, but from daybreak
I'll sleep another century."

" And I will talk before I sleep
And drink before I talk."
                                    And he
Had dipped the wooden ladle deep
Into the sleeper's tub of beer
Had not the sleeper started up.

" Before you have dipped it in the beer
I dragged from Goban's mountain-top
I'll have assurance that you are able
To value beer ; no half-legged fool
Shall dip his nose into my ladle
Merely for stumbling on this hole
In the bad hour before the dawn."

" Why, beer is only beer."

                                        " But say
' I'll sleep until the winter's gone,
Or maybe to Midsummer Day,'
And drink, and you will sleep that length."

" I'd like to sleep till winter's gone
Or till the sun is in his strength.
This blast has chilled me to the bone."

" I had no better plan at first.
I thought to wait for that or this ;
Maybe the weather was a-cursed
Or I had no woman there to kiss ;
So slept for half a year or so ;
But year by year I found that less
Gave me such pleasure I'd forgo
Even a half hour's nothingness,
And when at one year's end I found
I had not waked a single minute,
I chose this burrow under ground.
I'll sleep away all Time within it :
My sleep were now nine centuries
But for those mornings when I find
The lapwing at their foolish cries
And the sheep bleating at the wind
As when I also played the fool."

The beggar in a rage began
Upon his hunkers in the hole,
" It's plain that you are no right man
To mock at everything I love
As if it were not worth the doing.
I'd have a merry life enough

If a good Easter wind were blowing,
And though the winter wind is bad
I should not be too down in the mouth
For anything you did or said
If but this wind were in the south."

" You cry aloud, O would 'twere spring
Or that the wind would shift a point,
And do not know that you would bring,
If time were suppler in the joint,
Neither the spring nor the south wind
But the hour when you shall pass away
And leave no smoking wick behind,
For all life longs for the Last Day
And there's no man but cocks his ear
To know when Michael's trumpet cries
That flesh and bone may disappear,
And souls as if they were but sighs,
And there be nothing but God left ;
But I alone being blessed keep
Like some old rabbit to my cleft
And wait Him in a drunken sleep."
He dipped his ladle in the tub
And drank and yawned and stretched him out.
The other shouted, " You would rob
My life of every pleasant thought
And every comfortable thing
And so take that and that."   Thereon
He gave him a great pummelling,
But might have pummelled at a stone
For all the sleeper knew or cared ;
And after heaped up stone on stone,
And then, grown weary, prayed and cursed

And heaped up stone on stone again,
And prayed and cursed and cursed and fled
From Maeve and all that juggling plain,
Nor gave God thanks till overhead
The clouds were brightening with the dawn.

THE MOUNTAIN TOMB

Pour wine and dance if Manhood still have pride,
Bring roses if the rose be yet in bloom ;
The cataract smokes upon the mountain side,
Our Father Rosicross is in his tomb.

Pull down the blinds, bring fiddle and clarionet
That there be no foot silent in the room
Nor mouth from kissing, nor from wine unwet ;
Our Father Rosicross is in his tomb.

In vain, in vain ; the cataract still cries,
The everlasting taper lights the gloom ;
All wisdom shut into his onyx eyes
Our Father Rosicross sleeps in his tomb.

TO A CHILD DANCING IN THE WIND

DANCE there upon the shore ;
What need have you to care
For wind or water's roar ?
And tumble out your hair
That the salt drops have wet ;
Being young you have not known
The fool's triumph, nor yet
Love lost as soon as won,
Nor the best labourer dead
And all the sheaves to bind.
What need have you to dread
The monstrous crying of wind ?

II

TWO YEARS LATER

Has no one said those daring
Kind eyes should be more learn'd?
Or warned you how despairing
The moths are when they are burned?
I could have warned you; but you are young,
So we speak a different tongue.

O you will take whatever's offered
And dream that all the world's a friend,
Suffer as your mother suffered,
Be as broken in the end;
But I am old and you are young,
And I speak a barbarous tongue.

FRIENDS

Now must I these three praise—
Three women that have wrought
What joy is in my days ;
One that no passing thought,
Nor those unpassing cares,
No, not in these fifteen
Many times troubled years,
Could ever come between
Mind and delighted mind ;
And one because her hand
Had strength that could unbind
What none can understand,
What none can have and thrive,
Youth's dreamy load, till she
So changed me that I live
Labouring in ecstasy.
And what of her that took
All till my youth was gone
With scarce a pitying look ?
How should I praise that one ?
When day begins to break
I count my good and bad,
Being wakeful for her sake,
Remembering what she had,
What eagle look still shows,
While up from my heart's root
So great a sweetness flows
I shake from head to foot.

THE COLD HEAVEN

Suddenly I saw the cold and rook-delighting Heaven
That seemed as though ice burned and was but the
    more ice,
And thereupon imagination and heart were driven
So wild that every casual thought of that and this
Vanished, and left but memories, that should be out
    of season
With the hot blood of youth, of love crossed long
    ago ;
And I took all the blame out of all sense and reason,
Until I cried and trembled and rocked to and fro,
Riddled with light.   Ah ! when the ghost begins to
    quicken,
Confusion of the death-bed over, is it sent
Out naked on the roads, as the books say, and
    stricken
By the injustice of the skies for punishment ?

THAT THE NIGHT COME

SHE lived in storm and strife,
Her soul had such desire
For what proud death may bring
That it could not endure
That common good of life,
But lived as 'twere a king
That packed his marriage day
With banneret and pennon,
Trumpet and kettledrum,
And the outrageous cannon,
To bundle time away
That the night come.

THE MAGI

Now as at all times I can see in the mind's eye,
In their stiff, painted clothes, the pale unsatisfied ones
Appear and disappear in the blue depth of the sky
With all their ancient faces like rain-beaten stones,
And all their helms of silver hovering side by side,
And all their eyes still fixed, hoping to find once more,
Being by Calvary's turbulence unsatisfied,
The uncontrollable mystery on the bestial floor.

FROM
"THE WILD SWANS AT COOLE"
(1919)

THE WILD SWANS AT COOLE

THE trees are in their autumn beauty,
The woodland paths are dry,
Under the October twilight the water
Mirrors a still sky;
Upon the brimming water among the stones
Are nine and fifty swans.

The nineteenth Autumn has come upon me
Since I first made my count;
I saw, before I had well finished,
All suddenly mount
And scatter wheeling in great broken rings
Upon their clamorous wings.

I have looked upon those brilliant creatures,
And now my heart is sore.
All's changed since I, hearing at twilight,
The first time on this shore,
The bell-beat of their wings above my head,
Trod with a lighter tread.

Unwearied still, lover by lover,
They paddle in the cold,
Companionable streams or climb the air;
Their hearts have not grown old;
Passion or conquest, wander where they will,
Attend upon them still.

But now they drift on the still water,
Mysterious, beautiful;

Among what rushes will they build,
By what lake's edge or pool
Delight men's eyes when I awake some day
To find they have flown away?

IN MEMORY OF MAJOR ROBERT GREGORY

I

Now that we're almost settled in our house
I'll name the friends that cannot sup with us
Beside a fire of turf in th' ancient tower,
And having talked to some late hour
Climb up the narrow winding stair to bed :
Discoverers of forgotten truth
Or mere companions of my youth,
All, all are in my thoughts to-night being dead.

2

Always we'd have the new friend meet the old
And we are hurt if either friend seem cold,
And there is salt to lengthen out the smart
In the affections of our heart,
And quarrels are blown up upon that head ;
But not a friend that I would bring
This night can set us quarrelling,
For all that come into my mind are dead.

3

Lionel Johnson comes the first to mind,
That loved his learning better than mankind,
Though courteous to the worst ; much falling he
Brooded upon sanctity
Till all his Greek and Latin learning seemed
A long blast upon the horn that brought
A little nearer to his thought
A measureless consummation that he dreamed.

4

And that enquiring man John Synge comes next,
That dying chose the living world for text
And never could have rested in the tomb
But that, long travelling, he had come
Towards nightfall upon certain set apart
In a most desolate stony place,
Towards nightfall upon a race
Passionate and simple like his heart.

5

And then I think of old George Pollexfen,
In muscular youth well known to Mayo men
For horsemanship at meets or at race-courses,
That could have shown how purebred horses
And solid men, for all their passion, live
But as the outrageous stars incline
By opposition, square and trine ;
Having grown sluggish and contemplative.

6

They were my close companions many a year,
A portion of my mind and life, as it were,
And now their breathless faces seem to look
Out of some old picture-book ;
I am accustomed to their lack of breath,
But not that my dear friend's dear son,
Our Sidney and our perfect man,
Could share in that discourtesy of death.

7

For all things the delighted eye now sees
Were loved by him; the old storm-broken trees
That cast their shadows upon road and bridge;
The tower set on the stream's edge;
The ford where drinking cattle make a stir
Nightly, and startled by that sound
The water-hen must change her ground;
He might have been your heartiest welcomer.

8

When with the Galway foxhounds he would ride
From Castle Taylor to the Roxborough side
Or Esserkelly plain, few kept his pace;
At Mooneen he had leaped a place
So perilous that half the astonished meet
Had shut their eyes, and where was it
He rode a race without a bit?
And yet his mind outran the horses' feet.

9

We dreamed that a great painter had been born
To cold Clare rock and Galway rock and thorn,
To that stern colour and that delicate line
That are our secret discipline
Wherein the gazing heart doubles her might.
Soldier, scholar, horseman, he,
And yet he had the intensity
To have published all to be a world's delight.

What other could so well have counselled us
In all lovely intricacies of a house
As he that practised or that understood
All work in metal or in wood,
In moulded plaster or in carven stone?
Soldier, scholar, horseman, he,
And all he did done perfectly
As though he had but that one trade alone.

Some burn damp faggots, others may consume
The entire combustible world in one small room
As though dried straw, and if we turn about
The bare chimney is gone black out
Because the work had finished in that flare.
Soldier, scholar, horseman, he,
As 'twere all life's epitome.
What made us dream that he could comb grey hair?

12

I had thought, seeing how bitter is that wind
That shakes the shutter, to have brought to mind
All those that manhood tried, or childhood loved,
Or boyish intellect approved,
With some appropriate commentary on each;
Until imagination brought
A fitter welcome; but a thought
Of that late death took all my heart for speech.

AN IRISH AIRMAN FORESEES HIS DEATH

I KNOW that I shall meet my fate
Somewhere among the clouds above ;
Those that I fight I do not hate,
Those that I guard I do not love ;
My country is Kiltartan Cross,
My countrymen Kiltartan's poor,
No likely end could bring them loss
Or leave them happier than before.
Nor law, nor duty bade me fight,
Nor public men, nor cheering crowds,
A lonely impulse of delight
Drove to this tumult in the clouds ;
I balanced all, brought all to mind,
The years to come seemed waste of breath,
A waste of breath the years behind
In balance with this life, this death.

LINES WRITTEN IN DEJECTION

WHEN have I last looked on
The round green eyes and the long wavering bodies
Of the dark leopards of the moon?
All the wild witches, those most noble ladies,
For all their broom-sticks and their tears,
Their angry tears, are gone.
The holy centaurs of the hills are vanished;
I have nothing but the embittered sun;
Banished heroic mother moon and vanished,
And now that I have come to fifty years
I must endure the timid sun.

THE DAWN

I would be ignorant as the dawn
That has looked down
On that old queen measuring a town
With the pin of a brooch,
Or on the withered men that saw
From their pedantic Babylon
The careless planets in their courses,
The stars fade out where the moon comes,
And took their tablets and did sums ;
I would be ignorant as the dawn
That merely stood, rocking the glittering coach
Above the cloudy shoulders of the horses ;
I would be—for no knowledge is worth a straw—
Ignorant and wanton as the dawn.

ON WOMAN

MAY God be praised for woman
That gives up all her mind,
A man may find in no man
A friendship of her kind
That covers all he has brought
As with her flesh and bone,
Nor quarrels with a thought
Because it is not her own.

Though pedantry denies,
It's plain the Bible means
That Solomon grew wise
While talking with his queens
Yet never could, although
They say he counted grass,
Count all the praises due
When Sheba was his lass,
When she the iron wrought, or
When from the smithy fire
It shuddered in the water:
Harshness of their desire
That made them stretch and yawn,
Pleasure that comes with sleep,
Shudder that made them one.
What else He give or keep
God grant me—no, not here,
For I am not so bold
To hope a thing so dear
Now I am growing old,
But when if the tale's true
The Pestle of the moon

That pounds up all anew
Brings me to birth again—
To find what once I had
And know what once I have known,
Until I am driven mad,
Sleep driven from my bed,
By tenderness and care,
Pity, an aching head,
Gnashing of teeth, despair ;
And all because of some one
Perverse creature of chance,
And live like Solomon
That Sheba led a dance.

THE FISHERMAN

ALTHOUGH I can see him still,
The freckled man who goes
To a grey place on a hill
In grey Connemara clothes
At dawn to cast his flies,
It's long since I began
To call up to the eyes
This wise and simple man.
All day I'd looked in the face
What I had hoped 'twould be
To write for my own race
And the reality;
The living men that I hate,
The dead man that I loved,
The craven man in his seat,
The insolent unreproved,
And no knave brought to book
Who has won a drunken cheer,
The witty man and his joke
Aimed at the commonest ear,
The clever man who cries
The catch-cries of the clown,
The beating down of the wise
And great Art beaten down.
Maybe a twelvemonth since
Suddenly I began,
In scorn of this audience
Imagining a man,
And his sun-freckled face,
And grey Connemara cloth,
Climbing up to a place

Where stone is dark under froth,
And the down turn of his wrist
When the flies drop in the stream;
A man who does not exist,
A man who is but a dream;
And cried, " Before I am old
I shall have written him one
Poem maybe as cold
And passionate as the dawn."

MEMORY

ONE had a lovely face,
And two or three had charm,
But charm and face were in vain
Because the mountain grass
Cannot but keep the form
Where the mountain hare has lain.

HIS PHOENIX

THERE is a queen in China, or maybe it's in Spain,
And birthdays and holidays such praises can be heard
Of her unblemished lineaments, a whiteness with no
stain,
That she might be that sprightly girl trodden by a
bird ;
And there's a score of duchesses, surpassing woman-
kind,
Or who have found a painter to make them so for
pay
And smooth out stain and blemish with the elegance
of his mind :
I knew a phoenix in my youth so let them have their
day.

The young men every night applaud their Gaby's
laughing eye,
And Ruth St. Denis had more charm although she
had poor luck,
From nineteen hundred nine or ten, Pavlova's had
the cry,
And there's a player in the States who gathers up her
cloak
And flings herself out of the room when Juliet would
be bride
With all a woman's passion, a child's imperious
way,
And there are—but no matter if there are scores
beside :
I knew a phoenix in my youth so let them have their
day.

There's Margaret and Marjorie and Dorothy and
    Nan,
A Daphne and a Mary who live in privacy;
One's had her fill of lovers, another's had but one,
Another boasts, " I pick and choose and have but
    two or three."
If head and limb have beauty and the instep's high
    and light
They can spread out what sail they please for all I
    have to say,
Be but the breakers of men's hearts or engines of
    delight :
I knew a phoenix in my youth so let them have their
    day.

There'll be that crowd, that barbarous crowd, through
    all the centuries,
And who can say but some young belle may walk and
    talk men wild
Who is my beauty's equal, though that my heart
    denies,
But not the exact likeness, the simplicity of a child,
And that proud look as though she had gazed into
    the burning sun,
And all the shapely body no tittle gone astray.
I mourn for that most lonely thing ; and yet God's
    will be done,
I knew a phoenix in my youth so let them have their
    day.

UPON A DYING LADY

I

HER COURTESY

WITH the old kindness, the old distinguished grace,
She lies, her lovely piteous head amid dull red hair
Propped upon pillows, rouge on the pallor of her
    face.
She would not have us sad because she is lying there,
And when she meets our gaze her eyes are laughter-
    lit,
Her speech a wicked tale that we may vie with her,
Matching our broken-hearted wit against her wit,
Thinking of saints and of Petronius Arbiter.

II

CERTAIN ARTISTS BRING HER DOLLS AND DRAWINGS

Bring where our Beauty lies
A new modelled doll, or drawing,
With a friend's or an enemy's
Features, or maybe showing
Her features when a tress
Of dull red hair was flowing
Over some silken dress
Cut in the Turkish fashion,
Or, it may be, like a boy's.
We have given the world our passion,
We have naught for death but toys.

III

SHE TURNS THE DOLLS' FACES TO THE WALL

Because to-day is some religious festival
They had a priest say Mass, and even the Japanese,
Heel up and weight on toe, must face the wall
—Pedant in passion, learned in old courtesies,
Vehement and witty she had seemed— ; the Vene-
    tian lady
Who had seemed to glide to some intrigue in her red
    shoes,
Her domino, her panniered skirt copied from
    Longhi ;
The meditative critic ; all are on their toes,
Even our Beauty with her Turkish trousers on.
Because the priest must have like every dog his
    day
Or keep us all awake with baying at the moon,
We and our dolls being but the world were best away.

IV

THE END OF DAY

She is playing like a child
And penance is the play,
Fantastical and wild
Because the end of day
Shows her that some one soon
Will come from the house, and say—
Though play is but half-done—
" Come in and leave the play."—

V

HER RACE

She has not grown uncivil
As narrow natures would
And called the pleasures evil
Happier days thought good ;
She knows herself a woman,
No red and white of a face,
Or rank, raised from a common
Unreckonable race ;
And how should her heart fail her
Or sickness break her will
With her dead brother's valour
For an example still?

VI

HER COURAGE

When her soul flies to the predestined dancing-place
(I have no speech but symbol, the pagan speech I
        made
Amid the dreams of youth) let her come face to face,
Amid that first astonishment, with Grania's shade,
All but the terrors of the woodland flight forgot
That made her Dermuid dear, and some old cardinal
Pacing with half-closed eyelids in a sunny spot
Who had murmured of Giorgione at his latest
        breath—
Aye and Achilles, Timor, Babar, Barhaim, all
Who have lived in joy and laughed into the face of
        Death.

HER FRIENDS BRING HER A CHRISTMAS TREE

Pardon, great enemy,
Without an angry thought
We've carried in our tree,
And here and there have bought
Till all the boughs are gay,
And she may look from the bed
On pretty things that may
Please a fantastic head.
Give her a little grace,
What if a laughing eye
Have looked into your face—
It is about to die.

TWO SONGS OF A FOOL

I

A SPECKLED cat and a tame hare
Eat at my hearthstone
And sleep there ;
And both look up to me alone
For learning and defence
As I look up to Providence.

I start out of my sleep to think
Some day I may forget
Their food and drink ;
Or, the house door left unshut,
The hare may run till it's found
The horn's sweet note and the tooth of the hound.

I bear a burden that might well try
Men that do all by rule,
And what can I
That am a wandering-witted fool
But pray to God that He ease
My great responsibilities ?

II

I slept on my three-legged stool by the fire,
The speckled cat slept on my knee ;
We never thought to enquire
Where the brown hare might be,
And whether the door were shut.

Who knows how she drank the wind
Stretched up on two legs from the mat,
Before she had settled her mind
To drum with her heel and to leap?
Had I but awakened from sleep
And called her name, she had heard,
It may be, and had not stirred,
That now, it may be, has found
The horn's sweet note and the tooth of the hound.

THE SCHOLARS

Bald heads forgetful of their sins,
Old, learned, respectable bald heads
Edit and annotate the lines
That young men, tossing on their beds,
Rhymed out in love's despair
To flatter beauty's ignorant ear.

All shuffle there; all cough in ink;
All wear the carpet with their shoes;
All think what other people think;
All know the man their neighbour knows.
Lord, what would they say
Did their Catullus walk that way?

TO A YOUNG GIRL

My dear, my dear, I know
More than another
What makes your heart beat so;
Not even your own mother
Can know it as I know,
Who broke my heart for her
When the wild thought,
That she denies
And has forgot,
Set all her blood astir
And glittered in her eyes.

FROM
"FOUR PLAYS FOR DANCERS"
(1921)

A WOMAN'S BEAUTY IS LIKE A WHITE
FRAIL BIRD

A WOMAN's beauty is like a white
Frail bird, like a white sea-bird alone
At daybreak after stormy night
Between two furrows upon the ploughed land :
A sudden storm, and it was thrown
Between dark furrows upon the ploughed land.
How many centuries spent
The sedentary soul
In toils of measurement
Beyond eagle or mole,
Beyond hearing or seeing,
Or Archimedes' guess,
To raise into being
That loveliness ?

A strange unserviceable thing,
A fragile, exquisite, pale shell,
That the vast troubled waters bring
To the loud sands before day has broken.
The storm arose and suddenly fell
Amid the dark before day had broken.
What death ? what discipline ?
What bonds no man could unbind,
Being imagined within
The labyrinth of the mind,
What pursuing or fleeing,
What wounds, what bloody press,
Dragged into being
This loveliness ?

WHY DOES YOUR HEART BEAT THUS?

WHY does your heart beat thus?
Plain to be understood
I have met in a man's house
A statue of solitude,
Moving there and walking;
Its strange heart beating fast
For all our talking.
O still that heart at last.

O bitter reward
Of many a tragic tomb!
And we though astonished are dumb
And give but a sigh and a word,
A passing word.

Although the door be shut
And all seem well enough,
Although wide world hold not
A man but will give you his love
The moment he has looked at you,
He that has loved the best
May turn from a statue
His too human breast.

O bitter reward
Of many a tragic tomb!
And we though astonished are dumb
Or give but a sigh and a word,
A passing word.

What makes your heart so beat ?
What man is at your side ?
When beauty is complete
Your own thought will have died
And danger not be diminished ;
Dimmed at three-quarter light,
When moon's round is finished
The stars are out of sight.

O bitter reward
Of many a tragic tomb !
And we though astonished are dumb
Or give but a sigh and a word,
A passing word.

WHY DOES MY HEART BEAT SO?

WHY does my heart beat so?
Did not a shadow pass?
It passed by a moment ago.
Who can have trod in the grass?
What rogue is night-wandering?
Have not old writers said
That dizzy dreams can spring
From the dry bones of the dead?
And many a night it seems
That all the valley fills
With those fantastic dreams.
They overflow the hills,
So passionate is a shade,
Like wine that fills to the top
A grey-green cup of jade,
Or maybe an agate cup.

Why should the heart take fright?
What sets it beating so?
The bitter sweetness of the night
Has made it but a lonely thing.
Red bird of March, begin to crow,
Up with the neck and clap the wing,
Red cock, and crow.

My heart is in a cloud;
I'd let the whole world go;
My rascal heart is proud
Remembering and remembering.
Red bird of March, begin to crow,
Up with the neck and clap the wing,
Red cock, and crow.

The dreaming bones cry out
Because the night winds blow
And heaven's a cloudy blot.
Calamity can have its fling.
Red bird of March, begin to crow,
Up with the neck and clap the wing,
Red cock, and crow.

I

At the grey round of the hill
Music of a lost kingdom
Runs, runs and is suddenly still.
The winds out of Clare-Galway
Carry it : suddenly it is still.

I have heard in the night air
A wandering airy music ;
And moidered in that snare
A man is lost of a sudden,
In that sweet wandering snare.

What finger first began
Music of a lost kingdom ?
They dream that laughed in the sun.
Dry bones that dream are bitter,
They dream and darken our sun.

Those crazy fingers play
A wandering airy music ;
Our luck is withered away,
And wheat in the wheat-ear withered,
And the wind blows it away.

II

My heart ran wild when it heard
The curlew cry before dawn

166

And the eddying cat-headed bird;
But now the night is gone.
I have heard from far below
The strong March birds a-crow,
Stretch neck and clap the wing,
Red cocks, and crow.

FROM "MICHAEL ROBARTES AND THE DANCER"

(1921)

EASTER, 1916

I HAVE met them at close of day
Coming with vivid faces
From counter or desk among grey
Eighteenth-century houses.
I have passed with a nod of the head
Or polite meaningless words,
Or have lingered awhile and said
Polite meaningless words,
And thought before I had done
Of a mocking tale or a gibe
To please a companion
Around the fire at the club,
Being certain that they and I
But lived where motley is worn:
All changed, changed utterly:
A terrible beauty is born.

That woman's days were spent
In ignorant good-will,
Her nights in argument
Until her voice grew shrill.
What voice more sweet than hers
When young and beautiful,
She rode to harriers?
This man had kept a school
And rode our wingèd horse;
This other his helper and friend
Was coming into his force;
He might have won fame in the end,
So sensitive his nature seemed,
So daring and sweet his thought.

This other man I had dreamed
A drunken, vain-glorious lout.
He had done most bitter wrong
To some who are near my heart,
Yet I number him in the song;
He, too, has resigned his part
In the casual comedy;
He, too, has been changed in his turn,
Transformed utterly:
A terrible beauty is born.

Hearts with one purpose alone
Through summer and winter seem
Enchanted to a stone
To trouble the living stream.
The horse that comes from the road,
The rider, the birds that range
From cloud to tumbling cloud,
Minute by minute they change;
A shadow of cloud on the stream
Changes minute by minute;
A horse-hoof slides on the brim,
And a horse plashes within it;
The long-legged moor-hens dive,
And hens to moor-cocks call;
Minute by minute they live:
The stone's in the midst of all.

Too long a sacrifice
Can make a stone of the heart.
O when may it suffice?
That is Heaven's part, our part
To murmur name upon name,

As a mother names her child
When sleep at last has come
On limbs that had run wild.
What is it but nightfall ?
No, no, not night but death ;
Was it needless death after all ?
For England may keep faith
For all that is done and said.
We know their dream ; enough
To know they dreamed and are dead ;
And what if excess of love
Bewildered them till they died ?
I write it out in a verse—
MacDonagh and MacBride
And Connolly and Pearse
Now and in time to be,
Wherever green is worn,
Are changed, changed utterly :
A terrible beauty is born.

September 25, 1916.

SIXTEEN DEAD MEN

O BUT we talked at large before
The sixteen men were shot,
But who can talk of give and take,
What should be and what not
While those dead men are loitering there
To stir the boiling pot?

You say that we should still the land
Till Germany's overcome;
But who is there to argue that
Now Pearse is deaf and dumb?
And is their logic to outweigh
MacDonagh's bony thumb?

How could you dream they'd listen
That have an ear alone
For those new comrades they have found,
Lord Edward and Wolfe Tone,
Or meddle with our give and take
That converse bone to bone?

THE ROSE TREE

" O words are lightly spoken,"
Said Pearse to Connolly,
" Maybe a breath of politic words
Has withered our Rose Tree ;
Or maybe but a wind that blows
Across the bitter sea."

" It needs to be but watered,"
James Connolly replied,
" To make the green come out again
And spread on every side,
And shake the blossom from the bud
To be the garden's pride."

" But where can we draw water,"
Said Pearse to Connolly,
" When all the wells are parched away ?
O plain as plain can be
There's nothing but our own red blood
Can make a right Rose Tree."

ON A POLITICAL PRISONER

She that but little patience knew,
From childhood on, had now so much
A grey gull lost its fear and flew
Down to her cell and there alit,
And there endured her fingers' touch
And from her fingers ate its bit.

Did she in touching that lone wing
Recall the years before her mind
Became a bitter, an abstract thing,
Her thought some popular enmity:
Blind and leader of the blind
Drinking the foul ditch where they lie?

When long ago I saw her ride
Under Ben Bulben to the meet,
The beauty of her country-side
With all youth's lonely wildness stirred,
She seemed to have grown clean and sweet
Like any rock-bred, sea-borne bird:

Sea-borne, or balanced on the air
When first it sprang out of the nest
Upon some lofty rock to stare
Upon the cloudy canopy,
While under its storm-beaten breast
Cried out the hollows of the sea.

DEMON AND BEAST

For certain minutes at the least
That crafty demon and that loud beast
That plague me day and night
Ran out of my sight;
Though I had long perned in the gyre,
Between my hatred and desire,
I saw my freedom won
And all laugh in the sun.

The glittering eyes in a death's head
Of old Luke Wadding's portrait said
Welcome, and the Ormondes all
Nodded upon the wall,
And even Strafford smiled as though
It made him happier to know
I understood his plan.
Now that the loud beast ran
There was no portrait in the Gallery
But beckoned to sweet company,
For all men's thoughts grew clear
Being dear as mine are dear.

But soon a tear-drop started up,
For aimless joy had made me stop
Beside the little lake
To watch a white gull take
A bit of bread thrown up into the air;
Now gyring down and perning there
He splashed where an absurd
Portly green-pated bird

Shook off the water from his back;
Being no more demoniac
A stupid happy creature
Could rouse my whole nature.

Yet I am certain as can be
That every natural victory
Belongs to beast or demon,
That never yet had freeman
Right mastery of natural things,
And that mere growing old, that brings
Chilled blood, this sweetness brought;
Yet have no dearer thought
Than that I may find out a way
To make it linger half a day.

O what a sweetness strayed
Through barren Thebaid,
Or by the Mareotic sea
When that exultant Anthony
And twice a thousand more
Starved upon the shore
And withered to a bag of bones!
What had the Caesars but their thrones?

A PRAYER FOR MY DAUGHTER

ONCE more the storm is howling, and half hid
Under this cradle-hood and coverlid
My child sleeps on. There is no obstacle
But Gregory's wood and one bare hill
Whereby the haystack- and roof-levelling wind,
Bred on the Atlantic, can be stayed;
And for an hour I have walked and prayed
Because of the great gloom that is in my mind.

I have walked and prayed for this young child an
    hour
And heard the sea-wind scream upon the tower,
And under the arches of the bridge, and scream
In the elms above the flooded stream;
Imagining in excited reverie
That the future years had come,
Dancing to a frenzied drum,
Out of the murderous innocence of the sea.

May she be granted beauty and yet not
Beauty to make a stranger's eye distraught,
Or hers before a looking-glass, for such,
Being made beautiful overmuch,
Consider beauty a sufficient end,
Lose natural kindness and maybe
The heart-revealing intimacy
That chooses right, and never find a friend.

Helen being chosen found life flat and dull
And later had much trouble from a fool,

While that great Queen, that rose out of the spray,
Being fatherless could have her way
Yet chose a bandy-leggèd smith for man.
It's certain that fine women eat
A crazy salad with their meat
Whereby the Horn of Plenty is undone.

In courtesy I'd have her chiefly learned ;
Hearts are not had as a gift but hearts are earned
By those that are not entirely beautiful ;
Yet many, that have played the fool
For beauty's very self, has charm made wise,
And many a poor man that has roved,
Loved and thought himself beloved,
From a glad kindness cannot take his eyes.

May she become a flourishing hidden tree
That all her thoughts may like the linnet be,
And have no business but dispensing round
Their magnanimities of sound,
Nor but in merriment begin a chase,
Nor but in merriment a quarrel.
Oh, may she live like some green laurel
Rooted in one dear perpetual place.

My mind, because the minds that I have loved,
The sort of beauty that I have approved,
Prosper but little, has dried up of late,
Yet knows that to be choked with hate
May well be of all evil chances chief.
If there's no hatred in a mind
Assault and battery of the wind
Can never tear the linnet from the leaf.

An intellectual hatred is the worst,
So let her think opinions are accursed.
Have I not seen the loveliest woman born
Out of the mouth of Plenty's horn,
Because of her opinionated mind
Barter that horn and every good
By quiet natures understood
For an old bellows full of angry wind?

Considering that, all hatred driven hence,
The soul recovers radical innocence
And learns at last that it is self-delighting,
Self-appeasing, self-affrighting,
And that its own sweet will is Heaven's will;
She can, though every face should scowl
And every windy quarter howl
Or every bellows burst, be happy still.

And may her bride-groom bring her to a house
Where all's accustomed, ceremonious;
For arrogance and hatred are the wares
Peddled in the thoroughfares.
How but in custom and in ceremony
Are innocence and beauty born?
Ceremony's a name for the rich horn,
And custom for the spreading laurel tree.

   June 1919.

FROM "THE TOWER"

(1928)

SAILING TO BYZANTIUM

I

THAT is no country for old men. The young
In one another's arms, birds in the trees,
—Those dying generations—at their song,
The salmon-falls, the mackerel-crowded seas,
Fish, flesh, or fowl, commend all summer long
Whatever is begotten, born, and dies.
Caught in that sensual music all neglect
Monuments of unageing intellect.

II

An aged man is but a paltry thing,
A tattered coat upon a stick, unless
Soul clap its hands and sing, and louder sing
For every tatter in its mortal dress,
Nor is there singing school but studying
Monuments of its own magnificence;
And therefore I have sailed the seas and come
To the holy city of Byzantium.

III

O sages standing in God's holy fire
As in the gold mosaic of a wall,
Come from the holy fire, perne in a gyre,
And be the singing masters of my soul.
Consume my heart away; sick with desire
And fastened to a dying animal
It knows not what it is; and gather me
Into the artifice of eternity.

Once out of nature I shall never take
My bodily form from any natural thing,
But such a form as Grecian goldsmiths make
Of hammered gold and gold enamelling
To keep a drowsy emperor awake ;
Or set upon a golden bough to sing
To lords and ladies of Byzantium
Of what is past, or passing, or to come.

1927.

MEDITATIONS IN TIME OF CIVIL WAR

I

ANCESTRAL HOUSES

SURELY among a rich man's flowering lawns,
Amid the rustle of his planted hills,
Life overflows without ambitious pains ;
And rains down life until the basin spills,
And mounts more dizzy high the more it rains
As though to choose whatever shape it wills
And never stoop to a mechanical,
Or servile shape, at others' beck and call.

Mere dreams, mere dreams ! Yet Homer had not
    sung
Had he not found it certain beyond dreams
That out of life's own self-delight had sprung
The abounding glittering jet ; though now it seems
As if some marvellous empty sea-shell flung
Out of the obscure dark of the rich streams,
And not a fountain, were the symbol which
Shadows the inherited glory of the rich.

Some violent bitter man, some powerful man
Called architect and artist in, that they,
Bitter and violent men, might rear in stone
The sweetness that all longed for night and day,
The gentleness none there had ever known ;
But when the master's buried mice can play,
And maybe the great-grandson of that house,
For all its bronze and marble, 's but a mouse.

Oh, what if gardens where the peacock strays
With delicate feet upon old terraces,
Or else all Juno from an urn displays
Before the indifferent garden deities ;
Oh, what if levelled lawns and gravelled ways
Where slippered Contemplation finds his ease
And Childhood a delight for every sense,
But take our greatness with our violence !

What if the glory of escutcheoned doors,
And buildings that a haughtier age designed,
The pacing to and fro on polished floors
Amid great chambers and long galleries, lined
With famous portraits of our ancestors ;
What if those things the greatest of mankind
Consider most to magnify, or to bless,
But take our greatness with our bitterness !

II

MY HOUSE

An ancient bridge, and a more ancient tower,
A farmhouse that is sheltered by its wall,
An acre of stony ground,
Where the symbolic rose can break in flower,
Old ragged elms, old thorns innumerable,
The sound of the rain or sound
Of every wind that blows ;
The stilted water-hen
Crossing stream again
Scared by the splashing of a dozen cows ;

A winding stair, a chamber arched with stone,
A grey stone fireplace with an open hearth,
A candle and written page.
Il Penseroso's Platonist toiled on
In some like chamber, shadowing forth
How the daemonic rage
Imagined everything.
Benighted travellers
From markets and from fairs
Have seen his midnight candle glimmering.

Two men have founded here.   A man-at-arms
Gathered a score of horse and spent his days
In this tumultuous spot,
Where through long wars and sudden night alarms
His dwindling score and he seemed castaways
Forgetting and forgot;
And I, that after me
My bodily heirs may find,
To exalt a lonely mind,
Befitting emblems of adversity.

III

MY TABLE

Two heavy trestles, and a board
Where Sato's gift, a changeless sword,
By pen and paper lies,
That it may moralise
My days out of their aimlessness.
A bit of an embroidered dress
Covers its wooden sheath.
Chaucer had not drawn breath

When it was forged.   In Sato's house,
Curved like new moon, moon-luminous,
It lay five hundred years.
Yet if no change appears
No moon; only an aching heart
Conceives a changeless work of art.
Our learned men have urged
That when and where 'twas forged
A marvellous accomplishment,
In painting or in pottery, went
From father unto son
And through the centuries ran
And seemed unchanging like the sword.
Soul's beauty being most adored,
Men and their business took
The soul's unchanging look;
For the most rich inheritor,
Knowing that none could pass Heaven's door
That loved inferior art,
Had such an aching heart
That he, although a country's talk
For silken clothes and stately walk,
Had waking wits; it seemed
Juno's peacock screamed.

IV

MY DESCENDANTS

Having inherited a vigorous mind
From my old fathers, I must nourish dreams
And leave a woman and a man behind
As vigorous of mind, and yet it seems

Life scarce can cast a fragrance on the wind,
Scarce spread a glory to the morning beams,
But the torn petals strew the garden plot;
And there's but common greenness after that.

And what if my descendants lose the flower
Through natural declension of the soul,
Through too much business with the passing hour,
Through too much play, or marriage with a fool?
May this laborious stair and this stark tower
Become a roofless ruin that the owl
May build in the cracked masonry and cry
Her desolation to the desolate sky.

The Primum Mobile that fashioned us
Has made the very owls in circles move;
And I, that count myself most prosperous,
Seeing that love and friendship are enough,
For an old neighbour's friendship chose the house
And decked and altered it for a girl's love,
And know whatever flourish and decline
These stones remain their monument and mine.

V

THE ROAD AT MY DOOR

An affable Irregular,
A heavily built Falstaffian man,
Comes cracking jokes of civil war
As though to die by gunshot were
The finest play under the sun.

A brown Lieutenant and his men,
Half dressed in national uniform,
Stand at my door, and I complain
Of the foul weather, hail and rain,
A pear tree broken by the storm.

I count those feathered balls of soot
The moor-hen guides upon the stream,
To silence the envy in my thought ;
And turn towards my chamber, caught
In the cold snows of a dream.

IV

THE STARE'S NEST BY MY WINDOW

The bees build in the crevices
Of loosening masonry, and there
The mother birds bring grubs and flies.
My wall is loosening ; honey-bees,
Come build in the empty house of the stare.

We are closed in, and the key is turned
On our uncertainty ; somewhere
A man is killed, or a house burned,
Yet no clear fact to be discerned :
Come build in the empty house of the stare.

A barricade of stone or of wood ;
Some fourteen days of civil war ;
Last night they trundled down the road
That dead young soldier in his blood :
Come build in the empty house of the stare.

We had fed the heart on fantasies,
The heart's grown brutal from the fare,
More substance in our enmities
Than in our love ; oh, honey-bees,
Come build in the empty house of the stare.

VII

I SEE PHANTOMS OF HATRED AND OF THE HEART'S FULLNESS AND OF THE COMING EMPTINESS

I climb to the tower top and lean upon broken stone,
A mist that is like blown snow is sweeping over all,
Valley, river, and elms, under the light of a moon
That seems unlike itself, that seems unchangeable,
A glittering sword out of the east.   A puff of wind
And those white glimmering fragments of the mist sweep by.
Frenzies bewilder, reveries perturb the mind ;
Monstrous familiar images swim to the mind's eye.

"Vengeance upon the murderers," the cry goes up,
"Vengeance for Jacques Molay." In cloud-pale rags, or in lace,
The rage-driven, rage-tormented, and rage-hungry troop,
Trooper belabouring trooper, biting at arm or at face,
Plunges towards nothing, arms and fingers spreading wide
For the embrace of nothing ; and I, my wits astray
Because of all that senseless tumult, all but cried
For vengeance on the murderers of Jacques Molay.

193

Their legs long, delicate and slender, aquamarine their
     eyes,
Magical unicorns bear ladies on their backs,
The ladies close their musing eyes.   No prophecies,
Remembered out of Babylonian almanacs,
Have closed the ladies' eyes, their minds are but a
     pool
Where even longing drowns under its own excess ;
Nothing but stillness can remain when hearts are full
Of their own sweetness, bodies of their loveliness.

The cloud-pale unicorns, the eyes of aquamarine,
The quivering half-closed eyelids, the rags of cloud
     or of lace,
Or eyes that rage has brightened, arms it has made
     lean,
Give place to an indifferent multitude, give place
To brazen hawks.   Nor self-delighting reverie,
Nor hate of what's to come, nor pity for what's gone,
Nothing but grip of claw, and the eye's complacency,
The innumerable clanging wings that have put out
     the moon.

I turn away and shut the door, and on the stair
Wonder how many times I could have proved my
     worth
In something that all others understand or share ;
But oh, ambitious heart, had such a proof drawn forth
A company of friends, a conscience set at ease,
It had but made us pine the more.   The abstract joy,
The half-read wisdom of daemonic images,
Suffice the ageing man as once the growing boy.

1923.

THE WHEEL

THROUGH winter-time we call on spring,
And through the spring on summer call,
And when abounding hedges ring
Declare that winter's best of all ;
And after that there's nothing good
Because the spring-time has not come—
Nor know that what disturbs our blood
Is but its longing for the tomb.

A PRAYER FOR MY SON

BID a strong ghost stand at the head
That my Michael may sleep sound,
Nor cry, nor turn in the bed
Till his morning meal come round;
And may departing twilight keep
All dread afar till morning's back,
That his mother may not lack
Her fill of sleep.

Bid the ghost have sword in fist:
Some there are, for I avow
Such devilish things exist,
Who have planned his murder for they know
Of some most haughty deed or thought
That waits upon his future days,
And would through hatred of the bays
Bring that to nought.

Though You can fashion everything
From nothing every day, and teach
The morning stars to sing,
You have lacked articulate speech
To tell Your simplest want, and known,
Wailing upon a woman's knee,
All of that worst ignominy
Of flesh and bone;

And when through all the town there ran
The servants of Your enemy,
A woman and a man,
Unless the Holy Writings lie,

Hurried through the smooth and rough
And through the fertile and waste,
Protecting, till the danger past,
With human love.

TWO SONGS FROM A PLAY

I

I SAW a staring virgin stand
Where holy Dionysus died,
And tear the heart out of his side,
And lay the heart upon her hand
And bear that beating heart away ;
And then did all the Muses sing
Of Magnus Annus at the spring,
As though God's death were but a play.

Another Troy must rise and set,
Another lineage feed the crow,
Another Argo's painted prow
Drive to a flashier bauble yet.
The Roman Empire stood appalled :
It dropped the reins of peace and war
When that fierce virgin and her Star
Out of the fabulous darkness called.

II

In pity for man's darkening thought
He walked that room and issued thence
In Galilean turbulence ;
The Babylonian starlight brought
A fabulous, formless darkness in ;
Odour of blood when Christ was slain
Made all Platonic tolerance vain
And vain all Doric discipline.

FROM "OEDIPUS AT COLONUS"

I

ENDURE what life God gives and ask no longer span;
Cease to remember the delights of youth, travel-
wearied aged man;
Delight becomes death-longing if all longing else be
vain.

II

Even from that delight memory treasures so,
Death, despair, division of families, all entangle-
ments of mankind grow,
As that old wandering beggar and these God-hated
children know.

III

In the long echoing street the laughing dancers
throng,
The bride is carried to the bridegroom's chamber
through torchlight and tumultuous song;
I celebrate the silent kiss that ends short life or long.

IV

Never to have lived is best, ancient writers say;
Never to have drawn the breath of life, never to have
looked into the eye of day;
The second best's a gay goodnight and quickly turn
away.

INDEX TO FIRST LINES

THE END

PRINTED BY R. & R. CLARK, LTD., EDINBURGH

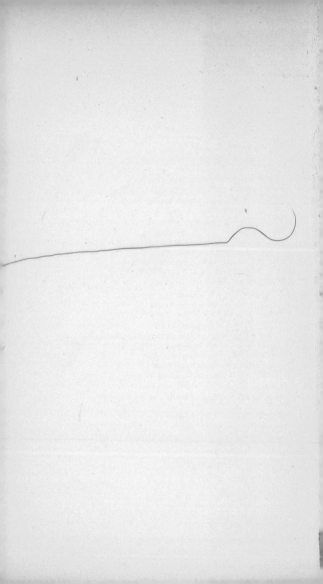